The Bles

MW01492378

Second Edition

By Jonathan Jones

The Blessing of the Thorn

Second Edition

ISBN 978-1-387-24531-4

Dedications

To all my brothers,

Thank you for letting me into your lives and hearts. Keep fighting the fight and be a stone of remembrance for future generations.

Contents

Introduction

About Perfect Hope Ministries

Perfect Hope is a teaching and discipleship ministry which was created to deal with the effects of sexual and relational sin within the Christian community. Within this context, the ministry addresses impediments and barriers to intimacy with God and others. The primary goal of the ministry is to provide biblically based tools and solutions which can be practically applied and promote honesty and openness through God's grace, mercy and forgiveness. The ministry exists to assist churches, families and individuals in the pursuit of purity, holiness and obedience.

The ministry provides 3 tracks of support for the Christian community. These are *recovery, intervention and prevention.* The material and programs for the *recovery track* is designed for individuals who have crossed over the line into sexual addiction through repeated falls and relapses. These participants have an individualized program and plan of action with an extensive follow up program. The *intervention track* is for those who have become convicted regarding their sexual sin and desire to begin a journey in pursuing purity before it advances any further. The *prevention track* provides tools and techniques for young parents to raise their children in the pursuit of purity and holiness.

Fear, shame, guilt and lies have kept the issue of sexual sin covered up or ignored within the Christian community far too long. In the past, the church has used fear and shame as a means of addressing this issue. These attempts failed miserably and only drove struggling Christians further into secrecy. Perfect Hope provides a message of hope, strength and encouragement. Our mission is to provide hope and freedom not only from sexual sin but from the burdens of fear, shame, guilt and lies. That hope is not based upon our ability because that hope will disappoint. That hope is based upon what Christ can do in restoring and healing our wounded souls and His Hope does not disappoint. Christ is truly the one and only perfect hope.

If you would have told me 20 years ago I would write a book, I would have laughed in your face. Well, here I am haven written more than one and now I'm coming back for my second edition with *The Blessing of the Thorn*. My father used to say "When you quit learning it's time to die." On a few occasions, I took that as a death threat because of my lacking interest in educational matters. As I aged, I realized life is a constant classroom where God creates and permits teachable moments. Since, the time I recorded my observations in the first edition back in 2011, God has been providing lots of teachable moments. This second edition has additional pages which include these learning experiences. So, I guess I'm still alive because I'm still learning. On a sad note, as I read back through my 2011 writings, I realized sexual sin has grown in its reach of destruction. On a happy note, I am finding more churches willingly and openly addressing this issue as well as preparing and equipping their youth with effective weapons. Let us pray the victories continue and we take back ground the enemy has taken.

Several years ago, I was visiting a local Christian bookstore and noticed something that was strange and out of place. I asked a nearby employee if I might be able to see the manager. In just a few moments the manager appeared and asked if he could be of assistance. I pointed toward the object of my concern and asked if he saw anything odd or out of place. He looked at the object and reported his inability to see anything odd. The object to which I was pointing was a sign hanging over a section of books that read, "Self-Help Books". Even now you may be asking yourself, "what's the big deal?'. My problem with the sign comes from the prospective that as Christians do we really need "self-help" books or do we need "Lord, I can't do this and I am broken beyond repairing myself, God help me!" book section.

If you obtained this book with the purpose of seeking self-help, then take it back because that is not the intent of this book. If you obtained this book and you are in a relationship with someone who struggles with sexual addiction and your goal is to gain enough information in order to fix the addict, then take it back. If you are a student or someone seeking clinical and statistical information based upon empirical research, then take it back. If you are a pastor or layperson seeking deep theological insight into the soul of the sex addict and desire scriptural reference and conformation for every principle presented in this book, then take it back. None of these pre-stated goals or objectives within themselves is wrong but that is not the intent of this book.

As I write this page I am now into my 6th decade of life. As I look back upon these years, I realize that through this span, sexual sin and the effects of sexual addiction has always been there. Over 4 of those decades have been spent in the area of counseling and mental health and sexual sin has probably affected more than 90% of the clients I have interacted with. These interactions occurred in inpatient, out-patient, residential and correctional institutions. During the early 90's, I begin working strictly in the area of Christian counseling and ministry. Prior this I had worked many years in the field of chemical addiction and was very familiar with the various types of addictions. At the same time, I moved into Christian counseling, I also begin hearing the term sexual addiction and the debate over whether it really existed. I was working at that time in a Christian inpatient program and I begin to see repeatedly Godly men struggling with the secret of sexual addiction. There was the pastor who was hospitalized for suicide attempts which were driven by his secret of sexual addiction. There was the former missionary who had been consumed by his sexual addiction, taken off the mission field and had lost all hope and purpose in life. Then there were the loved ones of the sex addicts who were also paying the price for the secret lives of their loved one. There was the pastor's wife with an eating disorder and multiple suicide attempts because of the shame she carried in protecting her husband's addiction. There were the female children of sex addicts that were now adults and struggling to deal with the abandonment of their fathers and his objectification of women. There were the adult male children of sex addicts who did not know how to love their wives as Christ loved the church and only knew selfish and objectified "love" of women. The list goes on and on. I realized through out these interactions, the church had a problem and we weren't dealing with it. I started to read whatever I could on the issue of sexual addiction, I asked questions, attended workshops and found opportunity to work in intensive workshops for sexual addicts and their wives. Probably, the most beneficial thing I did was to listen to these brothers and sisters in Christ that were in the struggle. Since that time in the early 90's I have listened to hundreds of stories from Christian sex addicts. These were not short stories but long stories that in some cases took days to tell. In those stories, they begin to teach me what they needed and how their relationship with sexual sin had developed and where it had taken them. This book is intended to present the observations, and themes these men taught me regarding their affliction. This book is not designed to create pity for the sexual addict or to shift blame away from the addict. There is no intent to try to diminish the addict's culpability regarding his actions. My hope is that, as a body of believers, we might better understand this assault from the enemy and stop shooting our sexually wounded or in some cases ignoring their plight.

My intent with these writings is first of all to be obedient to God. There have been just a few cases in my life when it has been very clear that God wanted me to do something. Writing this book is one of them. I do not know how well this book will be received or if it might even offend some people, but to be honest, I really don't care. I must first be obedient to Him. Secondly, I do not write this as a challenge or to disrespect anyone else's writings about sexual addiction. Once again, this book is about observations and themes that have occurred through the years of listening to Christian sex addicts. I do not write this to offend anyone's particular denominational beliefs. I am not a theologian and I do not want to add to or take away from anything in scripture. I will inform you in advance that not everything in this book is reinforced with scripture but hopefully none of the content will violate or diminish his Truth. My hope is you will read this book with an open mind and through the discernment of the Holy Spirit. Please, don't throw the "baby out with the bath water" because of some point of denominational contention within these covers.

Satan has used sex as a trap for Godly men since the beginning of time and God still used them after their sexual sins. Samson had a pattern of repeated sexual failures but God still used him and he even made it into the "Hall of Faith" in the Book of Hebrews. David was a man after God's own heart and through the lineage of his sexual sin came the Savior of the world. Solomon collected women like baseball cards and pursued pleasure to the fullest but he was allowed to build the Temple of the Lord. My point is if we don't come together as a body of believers then we will continue to lose the leaders and future leaders of our church and our families. Satan will continue to steal, kill and destroy by using his most effect weapon of sexual temptation. Let's draw a line in the sand and say, "no more" and let's take back what he has stolen. If the leader of the family falls then the church falls. If the leaders of the church fall then the community falls. If the leaders of the community fall then the state falls. If the leaders of the states fall then the country falls. Let's begin drawing the line today. If you are willing and open to listening, then we will begin.

Jonathan Jones, MS

President and Founder of Perfect Hope Ministries

Chapter One

Isaiah 43:19 See, I am doing a new thing! Now it springs up: Do you not perceive it? I am making a way in the desert and streams in the wasteland.

"Freedom. A word that Americans feel such a deep connection with, but seem to have such little comprehension of. Sexual addiction had its grips on my life for 20 years. For a 30-year-old man that number is haunting and large. Society and opportunity both gave me "freedom" to make the choices to lead a life full of sexual sin. However, the truth of the matter was my addiction was slavery.

My story begins, like so many, with an early exposure to pornography. Sometimes I hear of men who say early exposure was forced on them, but in my experience, I was seeking it for myself. All of my youth I hid what I was doing. Developing into adolescence brought more secrets and hiding. I lost my virginity in the upstairs classroom of my church in the 8th grade. What is even more hideous is the fact that THIS YEAR was the first time I ever told anyone. Through my whole dating life, I never was faithful to a girlfriend. I always kept girls on the side, in secret. When I was 17 my father/spiritual mentor died. My sexual sin deepened as I tried to seek my manly affirmation from girls. Going to college at a Christian school deepened my secret keeping. Hiding pornography, seeking secret places to do unholy things with women all feed into my addiction. This pattern held me hostage all through my early 20's.

I started to date the woman of my dreams when I was 27. The grip of my addiction was so great I couldn't step away from the lifestyle I had created. SLAVERY. I had a wonderful job and a beautiful fiancé by the time I was 29. My lies and secrets about my sins, and one in particular with another woman involved with my work, lead to me losing a job that I love dearly. After I was almost caught with that other woman, my wife, who kept me regardless, caught me with pornography. I was using pornography as a maintenance drug. She kicked me out of the house less after being married for 100 days. I had destroyed my career and the intimacy with the most beautiful and loving woman I had ever known. My addiction, my idol, my slave master lead me to pain, suffering, and death. Above all this had led to lack intimacy with God. It drove me directly into a cave. It was time to be redefined and reassigned.

I was staying in a hotel the first time I talked with David. I was so broken I could barely tell him my story. We began my restoration path immediately. I moved from a hotel to a friend's house for two weeks as I began my recovery. God began to show me the holes in my life that lead and feed my addiction. Addiction is your longing for worship gone bad. I had been tricked into thinking my life, which was seen as one of service to other people, had compartmentalized this nasty ugly part of my life into secret. One of Satan's biggest tricks, it seems to me, is allowing Christians to believe we know and serve Jesus except for this one little thing. That one little thing, whatever it is, grows and grows until we are no longer able to control it. Being a follower of Christ is a direct rejection of compartmentalization. There is no part of our life and brain that we can keep to ourselves. Restoration Path allowed me to finally see that Jesus Christ did not climb on a cross to make me feel bad for all the crap that I had done. He did it to set me free from all the crap that I had done.

Two weeks into my recovery my wife let me back into the house. My struggle was tested early and I experienced failures early. Secrets fueled my addiction. Telling the truth to my God, my wife, and my friends was a battle for me. During these recovery weeks, I decided to stop fighting it myself and start holding and trusting in God alone. The teaching of Restoration Path allowed the Holy Spirit to guide me to a place of freedom. TRUE FREEDOM. Proverbs 10:9 says "A man of integrity walks securely, but he who takes a crooked path will be found out." My wife found some of my sins out during this time. Finally, six weeks into my recovery I shared the entirety of my sins with my wife. With David in the room, she wrote down notes as I fully shared my history. She took the notes ripped them up and said we could now move on together. WOW. What an amazing woman. Now the freedom I was experiencing because of God's grace is starting to win back and define our marriage as well. Because of Gods truth I walk every day securely. True Freedom.

This battle has brought new life. Some of the brothers I share with on a weekly basis speak of good seasons in their battle with sexual addiction. I can honestly say I never experienced that. One of my lessons dealt with Paul discussing the Thorn in the Flesh and I was asked if I was angry with God for never taking this sin away from me when I asked. I had never really asked. However, my newly found freedom has allowed me to see things in a whole new light. Just because we are in churches doesn't mean we are seeking God. Just *because we attend Christian schools doesn't mean we are seeking God. A few weeks ago, I was walking down the Greenline in Memphis. This is an old railroad track that has been converted into a 6-mile walking and bike trail. I could see down the path a very long way in the current place I was walking. My thoughts drifted back to intensive workshop, as they often do, and I begin to think about my road ahead. As I gazed down the Greenline I had a thought that the road in front of me was long but the path was clear. There were no major branches down; I didn't have to cut grass or clear brush to continue my walk. I was walking on solid foundation, down a straight path where I can see clearly. All I had to do is stay on the path and continue to walk ahead. Our biggest problems come when we try and create our own path. God has made our paths straight and clear. Seeking him daily, our sometime based on my needs second by second, allow us to keep walking. Good seasons become lifetimes when God is the center of our thoughts and hearts. True Freedom*

I chose the verse at the top because my life was a desert, but God created a new way in me. Earlier in that chapter God talks through Isaiah about not letting the water overtake you or not letting the fire setting you ablaze. If you have been drowning or been on fire those are comforting thoughts. However, having a stream in the wasteland of the life you created for yourself is far more comforting to me. I am 10 weeks into my battle. The blessing for me is my restoration is not built on some "spiritual high" that will fade. God's grace is sufficient for everything that any of us are struggling with and whatever wasteland we have created he will give us a stream that provides life.

What we do with that life is our choice. God's grace is sufficient, but it's his truth that will set us free. One of my favorite worship songs says it this way "My chains are gone, I've been set free. My savior, God, has ransomed me. And like a flood, his mercy rains. Unending love, Amazing Grace". Today, I choose a true freedom."

Former client

What is Sexual Addiction?

Most Christians have a difficult time understanding how a follower of Christ could become a sexual addict. Because of this lack of understanding we often venture into assessing and judging those who are afflicted with this struggle. Due to this lack of understanding we often assess this person as not being saved in the first place. We may also decide they just lack the faith and strength to overcome this plague. Hopefully, in the next few pages we can address some these misunderstandings. I believe if we can take away some of the mystery associated with this sin then we can create an environment within our churches where we are no longer afraid to deal with this subject. Maybe, we can become the church which says "we can deal with anything with honesty and truth and through God's grace, mercy and forgiveness."

What is Sexual Addiction? Now we could go to secular publications and seek our answer and undoubtedly it would fit. We could do a public survey and come up with the most widely held opinion and this could suffice as well. The short answer; however, is that sexual addiction is idolatry.

Colossians 3:5 *Therefore put to death your members which are on the earth: fornication, uncleanness, passion, evil desire, and covetousness, <u>which is idolatry</u>.* (NKJV)

God hard wired into all humans a worship drive and he intended for it to be directed and fulfilled in our relationship with Him. Obviously, most of humanity has a misplaced worship drive. The same thing happens with the Christian sex addict. This is not a sudden or abrupt occurrence but one which is gradual and subtle over time. Our worship drive was formed and designed to be occupied by God and God alone. When the sharing of our worship drive is attempted then the process of instability or double-mindedness will begin. This also initiates the construction of an idol.

Anything we go to as a means of coping, escaping, or medicating, instead of going to God, can become an idol. Anything that fills all or a portion of our worship drive will become an idol. This is what the addiction becomes over time for the sexually addicted. It becomes a place to go where they can escape/reward and/or medicate as opposed to finding their refuge, reward and healing in the Lord. It doesn't matter if it is a larger idol that consumes your entire well-being or a small "pocket" idol you only visit from time to time. It is still an idol.

1 Kings 15:13 *Also he removed Maachah his grandmother from being queen mother, because she had made an obscene image of Asherah. And Asa cut down her obscene image and burned it by the Brook Kidron.* (NKJV).

Not far from where I live there is a family which has an almost 15 feet high statue of Buddha in their front yard. Now they have taken much time, money and care to landscape their yard to focus on the very large idol (or yard ornament as the city describes it). I knew someone once who that had a smaller version of this same idol on their coffee table. It cost much less money, and they spent less time taking care of it but it was still an idol. I would imagine you could even purchase such a statue so small it would fit into your pocket. Some sex addicts justify their use of pornography because they don't view it all the time. "I only view it a few times a year so I can't be an addict," is a phrase I hear a lot from men who are still protecting their idol. For the time being their use of pornography is a "pocket" idol. They are living under the illusion and delusion that they are in control. It is still an idol. My friend with the smaller statue had to dust and clean the Buddha several times a year and maybe light incense before it every now and then. It didn't take up much time, money, energy or space but it is still an idol. For some men, the idol grows into the Buddha in the yard. It is all consuming and everything in their life focuses upon taking care of and protecting this idol. Let me repeat, anything that you use as an escape/reward or to medicate instead of taking those things to the Lord can become an idol and fill our worship drive. For some people their big Buddha's are money, alcohol, drugs, success, work, affirmation of others and many more. For others, their smaller Buddha's are their children, T.V., toys i.e. cars, clothes, 4 wheelers, homes, exercise, etc.

Through the years, I have worked with about every addiction in the book and sexual addiction is different from any other addiction. Throughout this book, we will attempt to identify some of these differences. One of these differences is you don't have to acquire a taste for sexual temptation. Some alcoholics will describe having to acquire a taste for alcohol because at first it was unpleasant in taste and experience. I have never met a sex addict who had to acquire a taste for pornography, lust or sexual activity. As men, we are visually stimulated and this is how God made us. He intended for us to be visually stimulated by the nudity of our wives. So, when it comes to selling this idol it is an easy sell. I often tell people I couldn't sell a heater to an Eskimo but even I, with my poor marketing ability, could sell this idol. It is not like Satan is tempting men with taking a sharp stick and poking it in their eyes repeatedly with a promise of future pay offs. This is Satan attacking men in their basic design of being visual creations. This is an idol that produces a pleasurable experience from the onset. This experience can be so powerful that it very quickly masks the consequences and negative effects. This experience is also magnified and reinforced by today's culture of instant relief and gratification.

So far what we have looked at sexual addiction as an idol that is easy to sell because it is not a statue of a big, rotund, bald guy. It is the idol of a very attractive person who is perfect in every way. Imagine Satan as a door to door idol salesman. His promise is the idol will provide you with instant pleasure, excitement and stimulation. He also tells you it is free because you just need to go to the free web sites or just open your eyes to the world around you. He also guarantees that it will hurt no one because it is not like you are having an affair or seeing prostitutes and you are not taking food out of your children's mouths. It is the idol that keeps on giving with a life time guarantee. Pretty easy sell if you phrase it that way. He just forgets to tell you there are hooks buried in the idol that will sink its barbs into your body, mind and soul. During this "selling" period the sexual sin has not fully developed into an idol but it is an idol under construction. One of the goals of churches should be to address this while it is in the construction phase and not wait until lines are crossed and the hooks are set. In other words, let us empower our youth to successfully navigate a sexually fallen world before another generation is consumed.

I often call the addiction "The Beast" because it desires to kill you. It desires to slowly kill your marriage, your relationship with God, your spiritual growth and walk. Eventually, he wants your life. Because of the shame and despair that comes with being hooked, many addicts will consider and attempt suicide. Another analogy is to view sexual addiction as a black hole in space. Black holes will consume anything and everything that comes near it. Our churches are filled with men that are slowly dying and being consumed. In order to help free them from the hooks of this idol and restore what this black hole has consumed, we must first as a body admit that it is there. Secondly, we must be willing to come along side these men with truth, grace, reassurance, accountability, and restoration. In talking with Christian sex addicts every week, they repeatedly report one of their greatest barriers to coming forth with their struggles is how those around them will react. Their fears and sometimes their experiences tell them they will be abandoned, shamed, condemned and or punished. I once ran a Christian support group dealing with sexual temptations. Across the road was a conservative evangelical seminary. Some of the students who were struggling with sexual temptations would sneak over to the group. I say sneak because they all knew if it were discovered, they would be kicked out of seminary. These were not sexual addicts. These were men who wanted to be honest about the fight they were in with sexual temptation and find support. Sadly, the church historically has "shot their wounded" when it comes to sexual sin. Therefore, these men stay trapped in their own world of shame, loneliness and self-condemnation. As we progress through this book we will address how those around the addict can support his journey of healing. Once again, sexual addiction is an idol and an all-consuming beast that left unchecked will seek, kill and destroy not only the addict but those close to him.

John 10:10 *The thief does not come except to steal, and to kill, and to destroy. I have come that they may have life, and that they may have it more abundantly.* (NKJV)

We have looked at sexual addiction as being an idol, a beast and black hole. Now, let's look at it as relationship. This is a relationship with a thing and not an actual person but never the less it is a relationship. A relationship with a person or a thing is some thing or somebody in which you invest time, energy, focus and experiences. You do this with a thing as well as a human being. When I was growing up, we had very close relationships with our cars. They all had names and unique personalities. Sometimes you had to know their personalities to get them started. I continued this tradition into my adult life. Awhile back I sold my 1987 Toyota Corolla with 280,000 miles on it. Its name was Putt-Putt and I invested much time, energy, focus and too many to count experiences with it. Almost all of these experiences carry fond memories. However, toward the end of our relationship she began to take more than she gave so we had to part company.

The same thing is true with the sexually addicted. With some men, the addiction is the longest standing relationship in their life. If you would, visualize relationships as being on a straight line. At one end of the line is the beginning of the relationship and at the other is the end or conclusion. This line represents a time line and along that line are experiences that we share with that person. Some relationships have very short lines. An example of that may be someone you sit beside on a 2-hour flight and began a conversation. You never see this person again and so the relationship begins and concludes within a 2-hour time period. Other relationships are on a very long line. An example of this would be your parents, wife and children. For the most part the addict's relationship with the addiction is a very long line that began in their childhood or adolescence. There are some exceptions to this especially when it comes to internet pornography. Internet pornography can be the crack cocaine of sexual addiction. That's to say that crack cocaine is almost always instantly addictive. Because of the easy access to extremely intense pornographic images available via the internet this type of relationship can progress very rapidly. In the last few years I am seeing more and more 13 and 14-year-old males that are fully advanced sex addicts and this is due to their internet usage. Even in these cases there was already fertile ground for the seeds of this addiction to be planted. We will cover more of this issue in later chapters. For this discussion, we will view sexual addiction as a long-standing relationship with a very long time line.

The sexual addiction relationship line will have 4 sections. The first section will be referred to as the Pre-addiction section or the Seed Planting section. This section is also where the idol of the addiction is being constructed. Following this section there is a line that is crossed over which is the Loss of Control. After crossing this line, you are now in the area of Sexual Addiction or Sexual idolatry and this area is divided into 3 stages or sections.

(See Illustration 1)

Illustration 1

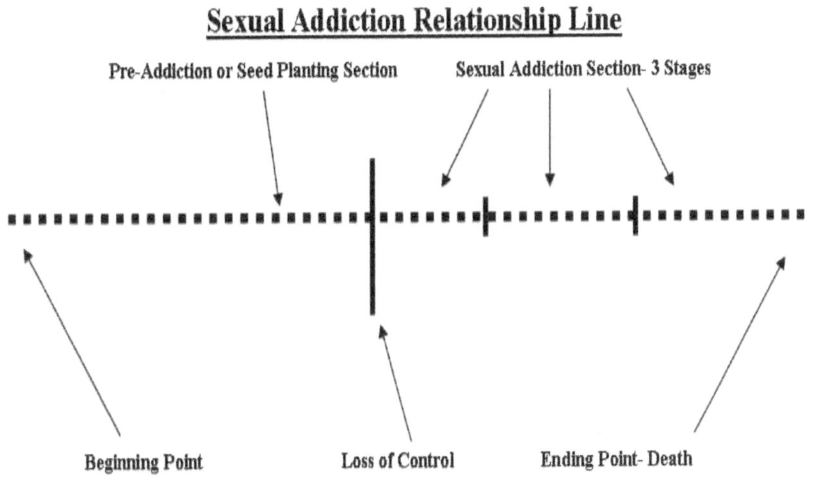

Sexual Addiction Relationship Line

Pre-Addiction or Seed Planting Section   Sexual Addiction Section- 3 Stages

Beginning Point   Loss of Control   Ending Point- Death

It is important to point out here that each addict's relationship with their addiction is unique and different. Each person's story and the seeds which are planted during the construction phase are unique and different. This issue will come up repeatedly throughout this book. Everyone, except Jesus, has a relationship with sexual sin. Some people never cross over the loss of control line and are able to set effective boundaries while other cross it very quickly. This concept will be important to grasp when we venture into the recovery process. There is no cookie cutter approach or one size fits all regarding recovery and healing. This is another reason why sexual addiction is different from other addictions. Each addict's relationship with the addiction is uniquely different and based upon the addict's needs, personality, coping skills, support system and other life experiences.

In order to understand the addict's relationship with the addiction we need to look at another characteristic which is unique to being a male. We have already discussed that men are visually stimulated and now we need to address the male's ability to compartmentalize situations and relationships in their lives. Let me paint another picture to demonstrate how men can compartmentalize. Imagine to your left there is one continuous cabinet and within this cabinet are several compartments. All of these compartments are connected. To your right are individual compartments that are separate and not connected to any other compartments. The compartments to your left represent the relationships and responsibilities in your life. For example, when you come into this world you may have individual relationship compartments for your mother, father, siblings and grandparents. All of these compartments are connected by the cabinet's design. In other words, if you get into a fight with your brother it will affect your compartments with your mother and father. We also have the ability to step out of these compartments to the left and into an individual compartment to the right. A surgeon, for example, may need to step into his surgeon compartment so he can put his complete focus into this activity. An athlete may call this being in "the zone". He is able to disconnect from all the distractions and focus fully on the job at hand. I know several men that have killed numerous other men. They performed these acts while in their compartment of being a soldier. Once they left this compartment, they never killed anyone again. The surgeon, soldier and athlete can later step back into their roles or compartments to the left, such as father and husband. This is not to say that females cannot compartmentalize, because they can. Females tend to be able to multi-task several relationships or situations. In other words, all compartments effect all compartments all the time. Women tend to see the "big picture" in relationships. The ability for men to put situations into compartments is part of God's design. If this compartmentalization is used with God's purpose, then this is where a man's vision, focus and leadership can glorify God, because he has a drive to accomplish what God has given him to do. An example would be Nehemiah and his drive to rebuild the wall of protection around the temple. That was the compartment God gave him and he was not distracted from that vision. In healthy marriages, these aspects of men and women complement each other. The man is able to keep the focus and vision of where the family needs to go and the wife is able to assess the impact that this has on the relationships around them.

Once again, Satan attacks men in their natural design and their ability to compartmentalize situations and relationships. Keeping this in mind let's return to our topic of the addiction being a relationship. We come into this world with a core set of relationships such as our parents and family. Upon each of these relationships we place expectations and needs. The more important the relationship is to us the more intense the needs and expectations become. As time goes on we may have several time lines of relationships going at the same time. As we go through these relationships we will experience two types of stressors. Many of these stressors are based upon the needs and expectations we place upon our relationships. There are positive stressors and negative stressors within relationships. Positive stressors are things like success, accomplishment, praise, adoration, validation, and many more. Negative stressors are failure, rejection, abandonment, disappointment, humiliation, loss and others. Both of these are natural events in anyone's life. Let's take the relationship that a male child would have with his father. As his relationship timeline progresses he will experience positive and negative stressors along the way. These stressors are intensified because of the expectations and needs he places upon his father.

Let's look at an example of a negative stressor. Little Bobby loves his dad and both he and his dad love baseball. Bobby is twelve years old and the all-star pitcher for his team. Today is the big game and if they win they will be going to the World Series. It's the last inning, with the bases loaded, and the score is tied. Bobby decides to try his new curve ball even though his coach, who is also his father, has told him not to use it. The pitch doesn't work, the curve doesn't break and he hangs a slow floater across the middle of the plate. Base hit, game over, they lose, season is over and the chances of going to the 12-year olds World Series is gone forever. Bobby is now experiencing a negative stressor because his perception is that he is a failure and everyone will reject him. He also has a need and expectation of comfort and reassurance from his father. Now, his father has a choice to make. This situation could be an opportunity to give Bobby life tools to put away in his life coping tool box and address his needs by pointing him toward the source of eternal comfort. Or he could give him the wrong tool or do nothing at all. If Bobby does not get the tools or his needs addressed to deal with this negative stressor or those that will follow, then this can be the place Satan comes into the picture. We know that God's timing is perfect but Satan's ain't too bad either. Many times, following these disappointments of life is when the child will begin his relationship with the addiction. Because, if there is no system in place to deal with these negative experiences or stressors, then as a human being Bobby is going to want to escape and medicate his painful feelings and unmet needs. I can't tell you how many stories I've heard from men where their first exposure to sexual temptation followed a negative stressor or a series of stressors. Because guess what? There is no failure, disappointment, abandonment, humiliation, rejection or loss in the fantasy world. I have yet to meet a human, not to mention a sex addict, that ever fantasized about any of these negative stressors.

Let's extend Bobby's story 2 weeks down the road of life. He is riding his bike down the road and notices a pornographic magazine beside the road. He has been carrying the shame of his failure for 2 weeks and needs some way to loosen the burden that he feels yoked to. In the eyes of these models he finds no rejections or looks of disappointment. He sees only acceptance and affirmation. Not only does he receive this message, he also receives an instant chemical release in his brain of dopamine. Dopamine is a natural chemical which is released from the pleasure area of our brain that makes us feel good. You see Bobby's dopamine level has been depleted for 2 weeks and he is yearning for a "feel good". He has also been carrying his disappointed needs and expectations. The longer he carries this neediness the more desperate he becomes. This incident may initiate the construction of his sexual fantasy relationship compartment. This does not mean that little 12-year-old Bobby has become a sex addict. It means that his relationship time line with sexual fantasy has begun. Instead of learning to deal with the hurtful and disappointing things of life and learning to take those things to God, he is learning to escape and medicate.

Now, let's look at the positive stressors in life. Let's say this time Bobby strikes out the batter and when he bats he hits a walk-off home run and wins the game. His father still has a choice to make in teaching his son how to deal with this situation. If Bobby learns that his acceptance, adoration and validation needs are only met through successful performance then he may begin carrying this burden. In this process, he may put extreme pressure and high expectations on himself in every situation to be successful because his entire worth and being rides on his ability to perform. I have worked with many successful men that never learned how to be "human beings" because they were defined by what they did and how well they performed, they became "human doers". The addiction relationship can find its beginning point here as well. (See Illustration 1) In the sexual fantasy world, there is no pressure to perform or get everything right in order to get your needs met. This time when Bobby finds the porn by the road, he sees in the eyes of the model a look of openness, which is free from criticism and scrutinizing.

You see, Satan's answer to these stressors is that he has a place, or a compartment, that you can go to escape and medicate these things. Satan's lie is that he has the perfect relationship or sanctuary where he can get all his emotional and relational needs met without fear of failure or rejection. This sexual fantasy world also gives an instant "feel good" response with the promise that it is a "victimless crime". Because as Bobby's life continues and he does not get the tools he needs to deal with the negative and positive stressors or the disappointments, then he goes into adult life with an empty tool box. In adult life, the stressors and disappointments do not go away but they intensify with more pressure and consequences riding on each situation. Because in adult life: it's not losing the ball game, it's losing your job and it's not the rejection of a friend but the rejection of your wife. As the stressors intensify, the need for higher levels of "feel good" chemicals increase and the need to escape the pressures of life multiples. As this intensity increases the "medication" that he once used no longer works and he must pursue higher levels and thus promoting the addiction's progression. In other words, the soft-core porn that he used during adolescence just doesn't work anymore. It is important to understand that this relationship becomes completely separate and compartmentalized away from his other relationship compartments. This will begin the secret, separate and protected world of sexual fantasy. This compartmentalization process will also initiate a system of delusional thinking. In reality it is delusional to believe we can actually separate ourselves or a portion of our lives from God. This delusional thinking is one that is attached to our sin nature and inherited from our original parents Adam and Eve who believed they could hide from God.

One more thing about little Bobby, he is a Christian, raised in a Christian home, and his father, the coach, is also a minister. He has been taught what is right by Biblical standards. He has never been abused or abandoned by either parent but in both scenarios, he is needy and Satan's attacking lie is he can and will address your neediness.

In either scenario, whether his struggle involves positive or negative stressors, Bobby needs a means to cope. In other words, he wants to feel better and gain some relief from these burdens. Satan may introduce this vulnerable young man to the addiction in various ways. It may be pornographic images on a friend's smart phone, an Rrated movie on free HBO weekend or an unsolicited "sexting" message. It could be something as subtle as an under-wear ad in a newspaper or magazine. Whatever the means, the seeds, or the beginning stage of this relationship has been initiated or planted. He will begin compartmentalizing or separating out his secret fantasy world from the rest of his relationships. He will also begin to protect this secret world. He begins to buy into the lie that his periodic viewing of these pictures is not hurting anyone because he is after all still a virgin. Through this process, he is beginning to protect and construct his relationship with his "pocket idol". He will rationalize, minimize, excuse and reduce his behavior. Because that is what we do with our idols, we protect them. As his relationship time line continues, he will eventually cross over a line where he begins to lose control. (See Illustration 1) He will first notice this loss of control in his thought life. Where in the past he could control his thoughts of lust in certain places and situations, he now finds that more difficult. He used to be able to control his thoughts while at church but they begin to creep in while praying or singing praise music. He used to be able to control his eyes, but now he constantly scans the room for visual stimuli. Now, he can't tell anyone because he never learned how to deal with failure and the disappointment of others. So, he covers it up and tries to survive and all the while slowly dying and consumed in the world of his secret sin. Not every scenario will follow this pattern because as I mentioned before that each relationship with the addiction is different. With some men, the relationship is introduced through sexual molestation and with others their self-exploration of their own bodies. The seeds can be planted in various means. In most cases, they come through the visual stimulation of pornography and with others the physical stimulation by others or themselves. I know of several cases where the seeds were planted through auditory means. These were young men who consistently heard sexual language or could hear others in sexual activity but never saw it. Once again when I say the seeds of the relationship, I am referring to the introduction stage or the pre-addiction time frame. We will discuss in a later chapter the fertile ground needed to receive these seeds. Not every child that is exposed to pornography becomes a sexual addict. Whereas every man is vulnerable to sexual temptation and lust but not every man becomes a sexual addict. One more note before we progress. Bobby's father could have done everything right in addressing his son's needs and Bobby could still have chosen to reject it. The issue and focus is not upon the father but upon Satan's response to our neediness and pain.

So far, we discussed sexual addiction as being an idol and a relationship that we feed, protect, and escape into as the stressors of life come upon us. There is one more way to view this addiction and that is as a thorn in the flesh.

2 Corinthians 12:7-10 [7] *And lest I should be exalted above measure by the abundance of the revelations, a thorn in the flesh was given to me, a messenger of Satan to buffet me, lest I be exalted above measure.* [8] *Concerning this thing I pleaded with the Lord three times that it might depart from me.* [9] *And He said to me, "My grace is sufficient for you, for My strength is made perfect in weakness."*

32

Therefore, most gladly I will rather boast in my infirmities, that the power of Christ may rest upon me. [10] *Therefore I take pleasure in infirmities, in reproaches, in needs, in persecutions, in distresses, for Christ's sake. For when I am weak, then I am strong.* (NKJV)

In 2 Corinthians 12: 7-10, Paul discusses some type of "thorn in the flesh". Now the truth of the matter is no one really knows what his thorn was and there have been numerous theories regarding its nature. Most theories center on Paul having an ongoing physical problem. Some examples could be malaria, epilepsy, migraines, or vision problems. However, let's look at this from a different school of thought. Let's approach this from the aspect of our spiritual flesh. Now what is our spiritual flesh?

Romans 7:5 *For when we were in the flesh, the sinful passions which were aroused by the law were at work in our members to bear fruit to death.* (NKJV)

Our spiritual flesh is a liar, cheat, manipulator, thief, murderer, adulterer, rapist, child molester and many more.

Jeremiah 17:9 *"The heart is deceitful above all things, and desperately wicked; Who can know it?"* (NKJV)

The Bible teaches that the "heart is deceitfully wicked" and our hearts are depraved. When we become Christians, we begin the process of sanctification. This is the process where our spiritual flesh decreases or dies daily and the Christ within us increases. We often refer to this as "dying to self". We are being formed and shaped into the likeness of Christ and to be set aside for a holy purpose. For most Christians, this information is Christianity 101. We learned it in a kindergarten Sunday school class. Now what do you think would happen if instead of putting to death this spiritual flesh, we protected, nurtured, and fed a portion of it by placing it in a segregated compartment. It makes sense that this portion might grow. Sexual addiction can become such a thorn that feeds upon our sinful nature or our spiritual flesh. Now, it doesn't feel nor is it initially perceived as a thorn in my sinful nature flesh because it feels good and buying into the lie that it is not hurting anyone supports our ongoing relationship with it. Instead of this separated portion dying each day, it is exacerbated, accelerated, fertilized, and magnified. The growth of this compartmentalized flesh intensifies because it grows in the darkness of secrecy and shame. We don't know what Paul's thorn was nor are we implying it to be sexual sin. But if we were to approach sexual addiction as a thorn in our spiritual flesh, we might have a clearer understanding of what God was trying to teach or give us.

In verse 7, of 2 Corinthians 12, Paul describes it as a messenger of Satan and a tormentor to him. I can assure you that sexual addiction is most definitely a messenger of Satan. You will be hard pressed to find a Christian man who is more tormented than a Christian sex addict. In verse 8, Paul describes that three times he pleaded with the Lord to remove his thorn. I cannot tell how many stories I have heard from Christian men who describe over and over again pleading with God to remove their sexual struggles, only to fall back into its grasp. Many sex addicts will try to remove their thorns through self-will, denial or becoming super-spiritual. Our own hard headedness or self-will cannot remove this embedded thorn. Maybe

Paul tried this approach because he was a pretty hard headed driven kind of guy. Others will just deny or minimize it as a problem all together. Some try to become super-Christians either through over involvement at the church or pursuing church employment or careers. This approach often leads to a works based righteousness. The problem is the sex addict continues to fail and he has to produce even more righteous works but he can never balance the books. What would happen if the sexual addict embraced his thorn and saw it as a teaching tool and a blessing from God? Now you might be saying to yourself or even out loud, "What? Are you nuts? Why would someone embrace their sexual sin? Isn't that giving a license to sin?" I am not suggesting embracing the behavior or feeding the flesh. What I am suggesting is maybe God has something to give or teach you through this tormenter of Satan. Maybe God can work through something that Satan intended for evil and turn it into a blessing. Now, don't get upset with me but I am going to leave you hanging for a while. We will return to the blessing that comes through the thorn of sexual addiction in a later chapter. We first need to understand the effects and dynamics of sexual addiction before we get to the restoration and healing part of the journey.

Well, let's do one more review before we move on to the next chapter. First, we identified sexual addiction as an idol, a beast and an all-consuming black hole. As we go through life we will experience stressors and disappointments. If we do not have the tools in our life coping tool box to deal with those stressors and disappointed needs then we may use sexual activities as a place to escape from and medicate our pain. Anything that we use as a refuge, medicate or sanctuary as opposed to going to God will over time become an idol. This in turn will subtly invade your worship drive and create a double-minded man. A man that has 2 masters will eventually love one and hate the other. We cannot serve God and this idol at the same time. The final result is a double-minded man who is unstable in all his ways and hooked by an idol that once advertised itself as only giving and providing.

James 1:8 [8] *he is a double-minded man, unstable in all his ways.* (NKJV)

Secondly, we viewed sexual addiction as being a long-term relationship. In the beginning of the relationship, the future addict believes this is the perfect relationship where all of his needs will be met instantly and no one gets hurt. Within the fantasy world of the addiction there is no rejection, abandonment, pain or failure. Over time the relationship begins to take control and leads the addict to places he didn't want to go. If we don't know how to get our needs met or how to deal with the stressors of life, we fall back in to this idolized perfect relationship.

Finally, we began to view the sexual addiction as a thorn in the flesh. This thorn exacerbates, accelerates and magnifies a portion of our sinful nature. It torments the Christian sex addict with the shame and condemnation of consistent failures to remove the thorn and repeated relapses into sinful behavior. With each failure, the sex addict's fear intensifies. If these flaws are exposed then he will be rejected, abandoned and punished. In order to keep this secret compartment of his heart hidden from others he will develop a false image that keeps others from getting too close. So, the final product is a Christian man with a façade of strength and an interior of fear, shame and condemnation. He may live in this dark secret world for many years until God exposes it and brings it into the light of his Truth. The truth about this idolized thorn in the flesh relationship is that the end result is death. With some men, this is a slow agonizing death which kills relationships with loved ones, time, creativity, money and eventually physical death. With other men, the process is faster and spreads like locust over the landscape of the addict's life leaving nothing but destruction in its path. Whether it is quick or slow the end result is still death.

Chapter 2

"I remember the feeling as if it were yesterday. I had it! My first porn mag! I was a freshman in high school and felt as if I had the answer in my hands. No longer would I wonder what a naked woman looked like. I'd finally know how this whole sex thing really works. I'd get to see pictures of it. I could hardly wait to get home. I was at an advantage. Nobody would be home for hours. I had all the time I thought I'd need to leer over every detail of every picture. I had an academic sense of what to do but is masturbation really just that simple? I open the magazine. Here goes nothing. The euphoria from the release overtakes me. I'm hooked. I walk into school the next day thinking I've arrived as a man. Little did I know I wouldn't figure out what true manhood is until my 30's. I spend the next few years of high school chasing that high. Off to college I go. The Internet is coming into its own and I had an email account that is absolutely bombarded with pornographic image after pornographic image. Still nothing beats that first high. I didn't know it at the time but I was an addict. I struggled through many relationships in my early adulthood. Rejection after rejection made my escape to pornography a habit. I didn't have to wonder what those women thought. Their eyes always approving. Never rejecting. I feared rejection so much I often, very painfully, broke off relationships so I could say I wasn't the one to get dumped. I would find a girl who inexplicably falls for me. I, in turn, fall for her. We marry after 2 and half years of dating and engagement. She never really asked about my past and I was determined to do better. Besides, I had a wife now. No need for porn. I was going to get sex whenever I wanted it! RIGHT?! Boy, was I wrong. Not only was sex infrequent she didn't ever seem to enjoy it. Immediately I start to withdraw. I needed approval. I needed to know I was desirable. The looks on her face told a different story. Here I was as vulnerable as I could be and she didn't even like it. I went back to porn. They never looked at me that way. But something changed. I didn't get the thrill I used to looking at porn. Now I needed a personal connection. I started texting a female co-worker less than a year into my marriage. It snowballed into nasty vulgar things that shouldn't be said period let alone from a so called "Christian Married Man". CAUGHT!! What was I going to do? I begged. I cried. I pleaded. I promised to never do that again.

She believed me. I was happy. But I never dealt with the idol in my life. 3 kids, a receding hairline, and many extra pounds later I somehow managed to survive. My daily use of porn returned with a vengeance. Sometimes I looked at porn 2 or 3 times a day. Still no connection though. I thought if I consumed enough I would find what I was looking for. Truth is I was eating from the wrong plate. I continued to drive a wedge between my wife and I with my sin. I kept justifying it though. Sometimes creating a fight just to be able to halfway enjoy the porn. She caught me again texting yet another girl. What do I do? I go into damage control. Testing the waters, I try to figure out what she knew. She stuffed it down for 6 months. I thought it was over and went back to looking at porn. Whew! That was close. Then she brings it back up. I'm pissed!!! "That's in the past!!" "I can't change it!" "You just need to move on!" Secretly I wondered if she knew. Then seemingly out of the blue she drops the "D" word. She asks for a divorce. I'm devastated. What do I do? What will people think of me? What about my kids? What will they think of me?

During a crisis, you will always revert back to your most basic form of training. I went to talk to a friend of mine who is a youth pastor. I lied to him about how far I had gone. I led him to believe that I'm not that bad of a person. Somehow through all of that my basic form of training was to run back to the cross. I rolled through so many emotions but there was something in my heart telling me I wasn't going to make it through this storm on my own. I got into counseling and even then, I wouldn't own up to just how far into sexual sin I was. But even still I found my identity in Christ. It was crystal clear. No longer was I a scared survivor medicating with pictures or videos of women or with relationships with other women. I'm a tender-hearted warrior!! Ready to fight!! I stand in the gap backed by The Sovereign God. Protecting those who need it. Steering those who need direction to God and telling them the road they are about to travel is full of pain remorse and sorry. Yes, I've lost my marriage, my reputation, my credibility, my dog and my truck. But God has given me so much more. I fought God about disclosing my past with my wife. I intellectualized it saying I've done business with God and that's enough. But I kept hearing this still small voice just asking the question, "Do you trust me?" Finally, I give in and do what was commanded of me. I didn't expect her to say anything other than what she did. She said that just made it official. In fact, I ended up coming clean to everybody I had lied to. I didn't expect very good responses. But something strange happened when I did. Each time I spoke to somebody asking for their forgiveness in lying to them they granted it. Many of them told me it changed nothing in our relationship except now we can build one on trust and honesty. Honesty truly is the way to receive the blessings God has for us in their entirety. I felt grace even greater fall down on me. Grace is so sweet. Mercy is met with gratitude. Forgiveness is freeing. For the first time in a long time I felt how deep God's love is for me. In Revelation 21:5 it says ..., Behold I make all things new.... God has renewed my heart. He has shown me grace in ways I never thought possible. He's shown me how He loves in very tangible ways through people on this earth. Because I've been given grace, my anger toward those who judge me is gone. I don't care what they think. It matters not. I don't need their approval. I have my Daddy's approval. 2 Corinthians 12:9 Each time He said "My grace is all you need. My power works best in weakness." So now I am glad to boast about my weaknesses, so that the power of Christ can work through me.

My circumstances have not changed and nor do I expect them to. But I have redefined them as a trial God put me through so I could regain my faith in him and spread The Gospel. I can't wait to see what God has in store me tomorrow and the next day and the next. But in the meantime, I'm going to be His. I no longer want to be my own."

Former Client

The Fertile Ground and Seed Planting

In this chapter, we will attempt to address how this addiction might begin and the fertile ground needed to receive the seeds of this sex addiction relationship. I need to remind you again that each addict's relationship with the addiction is different and unique. This chapter is a generalized view of how it might start. As we go through this chapter keep in mind we are covering the pre-addiction or seed planting phase of the relationship time line. We will cover the later stages of the addiction in other chapters.

I really like sweet corn and I like it fresh out of the garden. So, I decide I want to plant sweet corn and produce a crop that I can consume. Well, I take my seeds to central Illinois and plant my seeds in this dark, rich, fertile soil. There is a very good chance that I am going to get a very good crop of corn in just a few months. However, I don't really want to drive to central Illinois because gas is expensive and that sounds like hot hard work. So, I've decided to plant my sweet corn in my living room. I'll let sunlight in and will water and fertilize them repeatedly. The problem is my carpet is not fertile ground for receiving and producing sweet corn. The same thing is true for the pre-addiction or seed planting stage of the addiction. You need fertile ground to receive the seeds of the addiction.

Before we discuss the fertile ground, let's talk about the seeds. What are the seeds of this addiction? The seeds of this addiction are generally presented through 5 categories. These categories are: visual, tactile, auditory, smell and taste; with each one of these seeds carrying a sexual message. Now, I mentioned in the previous chapter that I would point out how this addiction differs from other addictions. Before we address the 5 categories we need to address what God's plan is for the sexual package. If you put all the categories together then you have a complete package. What God intended this sexual package to be is part of the spiritual bonding process that occurs within the boundaries of marriage. He doesn't want part of the package to be opened prior to marriage and the rest afterwards. He wants the best for his children and plans for husband and wife to have the full enjoyment of each other and not partial enjoyment. In Genesis 2:24, with the first marriage, God declares that man will be "united" and "become one flesh" with his spouse. Paul refers to this again in Ephesians 5:31-32 and also adds our union with Christ. In I Corinthians 6:16-17, Paul warns about "uniting with a prostitute" and the two becoming "one flesh". In understanding the Christian sex addict, it is important to understand the spiritual impact that it has upon the addict. There is a spiritual element to this addiction that is not there with any other addiction because of what God intended this package to be. In other words, this addiction and its seeds penetrate deeper than other addictions. I have talked with numerous men who have overcome multiple chemical addictions but can't seem to rid themselves of their sexual addiction. They used the same process and steps which worked with their previous addiction but the process fails to work. I truly believe this addiction goes to the core of who we are, our human spirit. In I Corinthians 6:18-19, Paul points out "all other sins are outside the body but sexual sin affects the body" and that the body is the temple of the Holy Spirit. Our sexual sin effects or invades the tabernacle of the Holy Spirit.

Now that I have your head spinning, let's return to the 5 categories of the seeds. As we look at each seed we will discuss God's plan and purpose and then give examples of how the seed might be planted. The first category is the visual seed. God intended for us to be visually stimulated as men by the nudity of our wives. These visual seeds can be planted by pornography, movies, or by the soft-core porn of magazines at the check-out aisle or the TV ads. Sometimes visual seeds are planted by accident. A young boy accidently views the neighbor dressing or finds porn out in the woods while playing. For most men, this is the most common seed planted because our society constantly sends out sexual visual stimuli.

The second category is the physical or tactile. God intended for the husband and wife to enjoy each other physically. The most intense part of this category would be full intercourse. When this occurs all 5 seeds are planted. However, sexual touching is also part of this as well. Sometimes the physical seeds are planted through molestation, or premarital sex. This seed can also be planted through mutual touching. At other times this occurs through self-exploration or self-stimulation. This self-exploration or stimulation may be a normal or natural act. Remember it becomes problematic if there is fertile ground to receive that seed.

The third category is auditory. There are sounds or auditory stimuli that is connected with the sexual package and part of God's plan. Seeds can be planted here through course, crude and sexual language or listening to others engage in sexual activity. I believe this area has intensified in the past few years due to the extreme sexual content of music today.

The forth category is the olfactory or smells. There are certain smells that are unique to this package. Often times this seed is connected with another seed such as the physical. A physical seed of premarital sex can be planted at the same time an olfactory seed is planted. This can be a very powerful but also subtle seed because the effect that smell has in linking us to events and memories of the past can be very intense. A certain smell of perfume or the smell of the room may link us to past sexual events.

The fifth seed is taste. An open mouth kiss is a sexual kiss and is intended to be reserved for marriage. Once again, this seed is often linked to another seed such as tactile and/or visual stimuli.

Some events may plant all 5 seeds at the same time and others just one. Never the less, you can find various combinations or links regarding these seeds. Understanding the seeds that are planted can give better insight into the plant that comes forth. This is the basic principle of sowing and reaping. If I plant sweet corn seeds, I am going to get sweet corn plants. If a person has a lot of auditory seeds, then the plant that comes forth may involve phone sex. If the seeds are more in the visual area, then the plant may involve pornography addiction or voyeurism. Let me stress, there is no way to predict how far addiction will go because "the heart is deceitfully wicked" and has no limits regarding sinful behavior. The sexual addict may believe that his appetite will remain only in the area of pornography because the "seeds" of his addiction were all visual in nature. This faulty belief system does not take into account the deceit in his heart and the concept of developing a drug tolerance. In other words, after a while, the porn won't give him the "the high" that it once did and he will need more to cover his pain.

Two other factors will determine if the seeds will be received: timing and the person's personality or bent. If I try to plant my corn seeds in Central Illinois in December, with the ground frozen, then that is bad timing. There are certain times in our life when we are more open and vulnerable to sexual stimuli. For example, the Jr. High years are a very vulnerable time because of what is happening chemically in our bodies, developmentally and socially. Most sex addicts will report an intense amount of sexual seeds being planted during their Jr. High years.

A person's personality or bent will affect the reception of these seeds as well. For example, some people are auditory learners and less visual. It makes sense that these men might be more receptive to auditory seeds. Some men's bent or personality reflects one of being adventurous and curious. The adventurous and curious male that has an initial exposure to pornography may be driven to explore more revealing venues of visual stimuli.

Ok, we've talked about the seeds now let's talk about the fertile ground. Maybe we can phrase it this way, "Why do some men become sex addicts and others don't?" "Does it mean that every 5-year-old that explores his body or sees pornography will become a sex addict?" The answer to the second question is, "No, of course not." The answer to the first question is more difficult to answer and will take a bit longer to address. As we venture into answering this question please keep in mind that we will not be shifting blame on to others or be trying to find healing through analyzing our past. We are addressing this question to better understand Satan's assault and in turn develop an effective battle plan to defeat him. In order to best address this issue or question of the fertile ground, we first need to look at ourselves as human beings.

We come into this world with a multitude of needs. We have physical, emotional, spiritual, mental and psychological needs and we don't have a clue how to get these needs met. Now what we desire is to have our needs met in a pure and perfect way with no disappointments or deficits. We want our needs met 24 hours a day, 7 days a week, and 365 days of the year. Well, the first people we look to address these in a pure and perfect fashion is our parents. Boy, that sounds like a set up for failure on the parents end and a place of disappointment on the receiving end. In other words, there is no such thing as a perfect parent. The parents can't meet the expectations of the child because sometimes they are not there. They may be other places because of work, church comments, divorce, illness or death. Sometimes this disappointment occurs because a generational pattern is in place where the parent did not get their needs met so they can't pass along something they never received themselves. Because a parent can't meet the child's expectation of their needs then disappointment will occur with the child. If there is a system in place to deal with these disappointments or stressors then the child might develop and grow effectively. This system should be one that has honesty, God's grace, mercy, and forgiveness as its foundation and one that is pointing the child toward a dependent relationship with his perfect parent, God.

Let's look at an example of an effective system. Little Stevie is 5 years old and afraid of the dark. His need is to be reassured he is safe and comforted in his fear. One night he calls out to his father to meet these needs. His father's response is to raise his voice and demand that Stevie not be a baby and grow up. Obviously, his need was not met by his father and at a minimum it is fair to say that Stevie is disappointed and intrusively wounded by his father's actions. If his father comes back to him with honesty and models God's grace by asking for forgiveness and Stevie forgives his father then there could be restoration and healing in their relationship. If the father then points Stevie to meet his needs through God by teaching him to pray and take his fears to God, he teaches a dependency upon his Heavenly Father. Stevie will need this tool because in the future his father will not be able go with him everywhere he goes and he needs to know that his Heavenly Father is always there with him and for him. You see the father wasn't perfect and in fact he even made a mistake but there was a system in place that pointed toward God.

Now, let's look at a flawed system. Let's use little Stevie's situation again but this time the father doesn't come back and ask for forgiveness and there is no healing, restoration or pointing to God. What will Stevie do with his disappointment? Not only was his need rejected but he was also intrusively wounded in the process. It is very easy to wound or crush a child's spirit.

Proverbs 18:14 *The spirit of a man will sustain him in sickness, but who can bear a broken spirit?* (NKJV)

A child's spirit can be wounded through 2 means: intrusively or non-intrusively. Intrusive wounds occur when something is coming at you and/or being taken from you. Non-intrusive wounds come from the lack of getting needs met or by abandonment. In the example of Stevie, he was wounded intrusively because his father's harsh words came at him plus his ability to trust his father may have been taken from him. If no one came to meet his needs when he cried out, he might have been wounded non-intrusively or through the abandonment of his needs. We all will be wounded, either intrusively or non-intrusively, by the people close to us. They will do it accidentally or intentionally. If this wounding becomes a repetitive pattern and there is no system in place to deal with these wounds, then God has given us the wonderful ability to survive. This survival system may involve a denial of one's needs because having needs means you won't get them met. And who wants to stay in a place of constant disappointment. Some of the men I have talked with have experienced both intrusive and non-intrusive wounds. Some have had few intrusive wounds. In other words, they were never abused physically, emotionally, spiritually, mentally or sexually. However, all the men I've talked with have experienced non-intrusive wounds. Most of these men were unaware of any wounding in their lives because they had no reference point. In other words, if they never had a need met then they don't know what is missing. The greatest area of potential wounding tends to be emotional. Let me give an example. Every young boy wants his father's approval and affirmation. If the boy never receives those from his father then a void is created and he begins to search for it. Whenever there is a void or vacuum that is where Satan will operate. You guessed it; there is no rejection or disappointment in the fantasy world of addiction. The world's answer to affirmation and approval is based upon what you accomplish and achieve with the constant pressure to perform. In the sexual fantasy world, there is never pressure to perform and there is always affirmation and approval.

Let me address one more area of wounding that we often don't consider and that involves how we can wound our self. Whenever we rebel against God and go outside his boundaries, we will become wounded. God wants what is best and safest for us. His boundaries, precepts and laws are there to protect us from our own rebellious sinful nature that desires to be god. The sexual addict may have been raised in a healthy family system where his needs were addressed and his disappointments dealt with openly and he may still choose to rebel. The story of the prodigal son presents such a picture. His family was healthy but he rebelled through his own accord and his sin cost him greatly. Sometimes the neediness and fertile ground is created through the rebellious works of the child.

Now, let's tie this back into the fertile ground that receives the seeds of the addiction. Our wounded spirits that go unattended are the fertile ground that receive the seeds. As a young boy looks into the eyes of his first soft core porn model, he does not see the eyes of anger, disappointment or rejection. He sees acceptance, excitement, validation and someone desiring him. As he enters his Jr. High years and begins to explore what the measure of a man is all about, he hears the locker room language. He hears the older males discussing their sexual conquests and determines this must be the measure of a man. The young boy, who has been wounded spiritually, becomes needier each day because he doesn't know how to get his needs met. As time goes on his need continues to increase and he reaches a place of desperation. Desperate people are dangerous. He is dangerous to himself because he will do whatever it takes to feel better and to fill his unmet void. He looks for places to escape and medicate. He tries various idols of temporary medication or escape but only one seems to bring a balm to his wounded spirit. He may eventually become dangerous to others because needy people will use others to satisfy their wants and desires. Adolescents are already self-focused and often self-centered. You combine this with their neediness and that is a dangerous combination. Over time, the seeds of the addiction are received into the fertile ground of the wounded spirit. This process is often what begins the construction process of building the sexual idol. Eventually, as the stress and wounds intensify the seeds sprout forth into a full blow addiction or a fully constructed idol.

Let's review before we move on to the next chapter. We come into this world with numerous emotional, spiritual, mental, and physical needs. We desire for needs to be met in a pure and perfect fashion so there are no voids or deficits in our lives. Our attempts to fill these needs through others fall short because they are flawed as well. When humans aren't able to fulfill our needs then there is disappointment. If there is no system in place to deal with these disappointments then we will be wounded. The wounds occur through intrusive or non-intrusive means. In Biblical terms these may be sins of omission or commission. This non-restored wounded spirit becomes the fertile ground that can receive the seeds of the addiction. Seeds left to grow are then fertilized by the stressors of life. These seeds can spring forth into the plant of the addiction.

"SEX ADDICT! He called me a sex addict. What a pompous, over educated jerk. Did he not know who I am? Does he not know who my father was? He calls himself a Christian counselor. I bet he doesn't even have a Bible. Just because he prayed with me doesn't prove anything. I told him I had confessed my sins before God and my wife and they had both forgiven me. I was standing on the power of the infinite and loving God to heal and deliver me from my affliction. Sex addict indeed! I am a child of the King.

I have to admit that he did stick to his guns. A lot of things he said really nailed me. He told me to stop hiding behind scripture and "Christian-ease". He told me I needed to get real and honest or I was going to die. He said my sexual addiction or idol would grow and consume everything in my life. No one had ever talked to me that way before. I told him he was crazy, questioned his salvation, to read his Bible and stormed out of his office.

That was almost 5 years ago. My wife has divorced me. My kids think I am a pervert. I was kicked out of my church. The very church my father started. I have been arrested for solicitation of a prostitute and I am all alone. I am staring a bottle of pills that appear to be my only way out. Then I remember something else that the counselor said. He talked about a hope that doesn't disappoint. He told me that God's grace was sufficient enough to cover my sins and get me through each day. He talked about from brokenness comes restoration and true healing. He said it wouldn't be easy or instant but it was worth it. He said I wasn't at that place of brokenness then. I am now. He said he would be there when I was ready.

Where did I put his card? Here it is. "Hello, yes, you may not remember me but ...."

Steve

Chapter 3

"Being betrayed by finding out an overload of new information about the husband I loved and thought I knew so well paralyzed me. I didn't even know what was real anymore. I was hurt, confused, in shock, and in a place of complete darkness. One thing I did know for sure was that I had to have a godly expert to show me the way to find healing. I thank God, He led me to Jonathan.

Jonathan was an amazing and compassionate listener. I felt immediately like he was on my side by the way he understood and validated my complex feelings of loss, grief, and betrayal. He helped me understand addictions, establish appropriate boundaries, and always pointed me back to the ultimate love and peace that only the Lord could provide me.

My husband was in sessions with him as well, and Jonathan was an agent for real change in getting him untangled from his sins of sexual addictions and alcohol abuse. One real fear I had was being burdened by hours of homework and meetings that I would feel pressured to complete to support my spouse in his recovery process. He took the focus off of any prescribed program and led me one conversation at a time whenever I needed it to find my security and joy again by turning to God.

I also deeply desired to move into the aftermath of our marriage crisis without lingering anger, grudges, bitterness, or mistrust. The godly counsel I received has helped me through the process of forgiveness and restoration once I had proof of real and lasting change.

My husband and I renewed our vows and started over with a new marriage after working with Jonathan this year. The Lord has blessed us inexplicably not only as a couple but also our entire family through Jonathan's ministry. Thankfully I also learned afresh to live each day with my ultimate trust not in people, but in my God who is my strength, shield, rock, security, good name, joy, salvation, and hope for tomorrow."

<u>*The Plant Comes Forth and the Stages of the Addiction*</u>

In this chapter, we will discuss the different stages of sexual addiction. It might be even more appropriate to define this as the progressive stages of sexual sin development. Just as a plant comes forth from a seed and emerges from the ground, so emerges the plant of sexual addiction. As I mentioned in the introduction, this book is not intended to be a clinical manual or to displace, discredit, or invalidate clinical research studies. This information or perspective is taken from observations, and discussions with hundreds of Christian sexually addicted men that I have interacted with throughout the years. These stages will differ from other resources that you may have read. I believe that some of these differences occur in how sexual addiction affects Christian men differently than non-Christian men. These stages also differ because they are related to the progression of our sin and not through a clinical model. Some of the obvious differences are that the Christian man has experienced periodic intimacy with God and the freedom that comes with having your sins forgiven and being washed of your iniquities. The non-Christian has never experienced these things and therefore has never known a sense of loss or separation from God. You cannot miss something you never had. The most miserable person you will ever meet is a Christian man struggling with sexual addiction because of this separation and tremendous shame he is carrying. The Christian struggler may reach greater levels of shame at a lower level of their addiction than the non-Christian experiences at more advanced levels. This is in part due to the Christian sex addict's rebellion from God and the lack of response to the Holy Spirit's conviction.

Remember each man's relationship with sexual sin is different and that is also the same for the sex addict. Some men may stay in stage one for their entire life and never progress while others don't pause at the first and progress very rapidly into the other stages. Some of this progression or lack of can be explained by the types of seeds that were planted, the timing of the seeds planted and the intensity of the seeds planted. In other words, the earlier a child is exposed to sexual stimuli and the more intense the stimuli, the more damage this can do to the child. However, there are exceptions to this generalization as well. If we were defining the stages of alcoholism this process could be fairly easily defined and each stage very clear but this will not be the case with sexual addiction. With all this being said, I will present what I have discovered. I will define it as the three stages of sexual addiction for the Christian sex addict.

Illustration 2

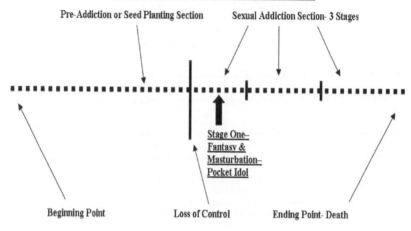

Stage One: Fantasy and Masturbation / Pocket Idol

Stage One: Fantasy and Masturbation / Pocket Idol

We will refer to this stage as the fantasy and masturbation stage. The addiction is now a "pocket idol". This stage probably has the highest population of addicts and because it is a pocket idol, it is easy to hide, protect and rationalize away the consequences. This stage does not involve physical contact or the direct victimization of others. The stage one addict seeks visual stimuli and self-gratification. His visual stimuli can cover a wide range. This range can cover mentally undressing women in public to hard core pornography. I had a man tell me years ago that he didn't need pornography because what he could produce in his mind was a whole lot better than what he could find in a magazine. Men have been producing porn in their minds for thousands of years, well before Guttenberg invented the press. This first idol stage is very easy to protect because this is the ultimate safe sex. He believes he is safe from: rejection, failure, disease, premarital sex, extra-marital sex and from hurting anyone.

His relationship with his idol sounds something like this: "Hey, it's not like I'm out sleeping around, I just have a higher sex drive than my wife, it's not like I am taking away anything from my family or God because I just go to the free sites, it's ok to look as long you don't touch. I have a lot of stress in my life and its ok as long as I just fantasize about my wife or I just use it to help me go to sleep." Be careful because if any of these reasons make too much sense to you then you could be constructing an idol or a stage one addict. A Christian sex addict can stay in this stage his entire life or he can move very rapidly through it and there is no way to predict its progression or lack of. I mentioned a moment ago the acting out in this stage involves only the addict and the use of masturbation. There is one exception to this however. I believe a majority of married stage one addicts act out with their wives as well. Let me give you an example. Remember little 12-year-old Bobby from the baseball team? Well, Bobby is now married with a very beautiful wife and a one year old son. Bobby is finishing up seminary and works part time as a youth minister. He is also a stage one sex addict that views porn late at night after he studies and his wife is asleep. He also struggles mentally by sexually objectifying co-eds in his seminary classes. His frequency of acting out with himself is 2-3 times per week. He justifies this behavior by believing his sex drive is higher than his wife, he does not want to wake her up to have sex and she is too tired and busy taking care of their toddler. He is also acting out with his wife 3 times per week through sexual intercourse. There are two reasons this is acting out. First of all, Bobby is visually stimulated all day long by attractive females in his classes and comes home in the evening and "uses" his wife sexually. He is not stimulated by his wife's beauty but by the lust he has built up all day long. I am not saying Bobby fantasizes about other women during sex, even though this does occur. I am saying he is "using" her to act out chemically. Love is never using someone else. It is always giving of one's self. Lust is always about using and never about giving.

The second reason is Bobby and his wife do not have emotional and spiritual intimacy. If they did have emotional and spiritual intimacy then they would be able to deal with his sexual addiction openly and honestly. Bobby can't have spiritual intimacy with his wife because he has an idol in his life and therefore can't have full intimacy with God. Without the foundation of spiritual and emotional intimacy then Bobby is just using his wife as a chemical high or release. His wife desires the emotional and spiritual intimacy but this terrifies Bobby because getting close may mean getting hurt and he never learned how to deal with hurt or pain. Most often the wife of a stage one addict will withdraw from sexual activity with their husbands because in her spirit she feels used but she is unable to intellectually grasp why she does not desire her husband. The husband interprets this as rejection and retreats further into his fantasy world of the addiction where there is no rejection. Many wives of sex addicts will blame themselves and feel guilty because of their lack of desire for their husband. Some will force themselves to be sexual with their husbands because it is the biblical thing to do. Little does she know that she is competing with the magical lady of the fantasy world and she will never measure up. However, most wives will find ways to avoid sex because of the emotional pain that comes with it. She will often find solace in her children, church activities, school and social functions. As the wife moves more into these areas to find purpose and meaning, the addict feels more abandonment and frustration. These patterns will continue for years until God exposes the true nature of the family's problem.

One of the most powerful lies the stage one addict believes is he is not hurting anyone, and therefore his actions are like a victimless crime. In situations where the addict is married, we have already discussed how he uses his wife. The principle of using one's wife does not fit into God's job description for the husband.

Ephesians 5:25 *Husbands, love your wives, just as Christ also loved the church and gave Himself for her*, (NKJV)

This involves loving sacrificially and not selfishly. No matter how you turn it, sexual addiction is selfish. The unmarried stage one sex addict may justify his use of fantasy and masturbation because he is not using a woman. Every time a man lusts after a female he is using her for his own gratification and fails to see her as a person that is valuable and loved by God. A sobering phrase that sticks in my head is, "that is somebody's daughter." And that carries a lot of weight for me because I have a daughter.

In reading this you may think that I am being too rigid or puritanical in my approach. But God has called us to be a set apart people that pursue holiness and purity. We live in a world that has lowered the bar of morality and colored areas of purity grey. As

God's people, we must raise the bar and bring every thought captive and bring them into obedience to God's standard. When Lot left the protection of his wiser and older Uncle Abram, he could have settled anywhere he wanted but he chose to face his tent toward Sodom. In other words, he faced temptation and before long he was living in Sodom. If your eyes continue to face temptation you will eventually cross lines that you never thought you would cross. We are instructed to flee temptation and not sit in front of it or invite it into our house. The more we compromise the line of purity, the easier it becomes to quench the conviction of the Holy Spirit.

Compromising becomes a habitual way of life and future lines become easier to cross.

Ill. 3

Sexual Addiction Relationship Line

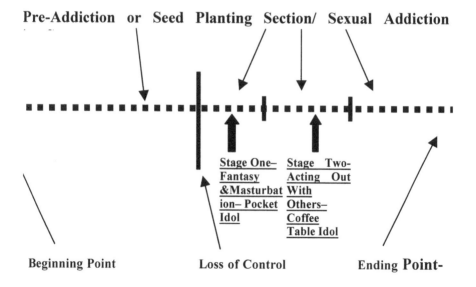

Stage Two: Acting out with others / Coffee Table Idol

If the addiction progresses into the second stage, it will now involve other people. The idol has now grown into the "coffee table idol" and will demand and take more from the addict. The black hole of his addiction will intensify and consume more of his principles and integrity. Just as in stage one, the second stage can be demonstrated in a wide range of behaviors. The behavior can range from inappropriate touching of others to multiple affairs. Most fetishes will begin in stage 1 in the fantasy or the mind of the addict and are carried out in stages 2 and 3.   For example, the fetish of exposing oneself initiates in the mind of a stage 1 addict and progresses into the using or victimization of others in the latter stages. If and when the addict moves into this stage, his "drug of choice" now changes. This is like a drug addict going from marijuana to cocaine. That is to say his drug of choice has shifted or intensified from marijuana to cocaine. When the sex addict shifts to this stage he moves from the drug of masturbation to the drug of sex with other women/men. When his "drug of choice" shifts then the addict will not stop his stage one activity but it will become his "maintenance drug". In other words, if a stage 2 addict can't find someone to have sex with him, which is his drug of choice, then he can fall back on his maintenance drug of fantasy and masturbation. Many stage 2 addicts will convince themselves they are sober if they only act out with themselves. They are only maintaining their relationship with their addiction until they can obtain their drug of choice.

Stage 2 addicts will also experience a shift in their "radar". A stage 1 addict's radar is attuned to pick up visual stimuli. A stage 2 addict's radar is attuned to find women that will act out with him sexually as well as visual stimuli. When asking a stage 2 addict how he knew a person would act out with him, he will generally describe recognizing this through eye contact. You can place a fully advanced stage 2 addict in a room with 100 women and only one of those women is willing to have sex with him and he will find her. There again his radar is attuned to finding willing or sometimes vulnerable women. During the seed planting time of his addiction and the fantasies of his stage 1, he was developing a "magical woman". In stage 2 he begins to pursue and find the magical women in flesh. The stage 2 addict cannot bring this magical woman into reality because she will not survive. For example, the stage 2 addict that has an ongoing affair does not deal with reality in this relationship. He does not deal with the reality of the world like; paying bills, sick kids, cars needing repairs and many other stressors of life. You see affairs and one night stands are still in the compartmentalized fantasy world. When reality creeps into the world of his affair then the addict will move on because he can't deal with reality and continues to chase after the magical woman that can meet all his needs. The stage 2 addict will continue with his Ecclesiastical chase for contentment just as a gambling addict chases the next big score. Please keep in mind that every addict's relationship with his addiction is different and not all men will reach stage 2 and some will bi-pass it and go straight to stage 3.

Let's return back to Bobby's story and how someone might progress to stage 2. Bobby has now finished his schooling and works full time as the youth pastor for an active and growing church. He and his wife now have 2 children and are expecting their third in just a few months. Behind their image of the perfect Christian family, the secret of his sexual addiction continues. He continues to view porn late at night and also at his office at the church. He has also developed a work-a-holic tendency at church. In his distorted thinking, he believes his good works at the church can balance out the shame that he carries. His secondary approval addiction intensifies as his failures with his sexual sin continue. In order to deal with her feelings of guilt, shame and insecurity, his wife's world revolves around her children. She has also developed an eating disorder and uses over eating to medicate her pain and despair. Bobby is frustrated with his wife because she gives all her attention, time and focus to the kids and he gets the left overs at best. He no longer desires his wife sexually and resents her for her weight gain. Because there is no emotional or spiritual intimacy, they are not able to discuss or deal with their negative feelings. Bobby is also feeling pressure at work to meet the needs of the youth in order to make everyone happy. Remember Bobby never learned to deal with the stressors of life. The stressors have intensified and the steady use of porn is just not enough medication to cover his stressors at home and work. Remember God's timing is perfect but Satan's ain't too bad either. Bobby is very needy at this point and has been for many years. In fact, he is past needy and is now desperate and desperate people are dangerous. In Satan's timing, he may introduce 2 desperate people to each other and the results are dangerous and deadly. Bobby has begun to interact with a very needy single mother of a child in his youth group. Under the umbrella of ministering to her, she shares her troubles with the understanding Bobby. She thinks he is the greatest because he understands and relates to her pain and loneliness. Their relationship begins as an emotional affair where they are sharing their hearts with each other. It appears they are experiencing spiritual and emotional intimacy but they aren't because it is only a counterfeit of the real thing. Bobby cannot discern that it is counterfeit because it is the Holy Spirit that gives discernment regarding what is from God and what is fake. Bobby has been running from God and the prompting of the Holy Spirit for a long time. You cannot hear the still small voice or whisper of God when you are running. In this emotional affair Bobby feels needed, wanted, and affirmed by an attractive woman. Before long the relationship becomes physical. He feels guilty but he will also justify his behavior by blaming his wife, the church's demands upon him and ultimately God because He is one who gave him this sorry life anyway. He will also compartmentalize this affair apart from the rest of his life because he is well practiced having done this with his porn use for years. This affair may be very short term or it could go on for years. Either way Bobby has crossed over a line from stage 1 to stage 2. Once a line is compromised, it easier to cross it again and again. Bobby is now having an affair with his magical lady. If he tries to bring this fantasy relationship into reality it will not survive. That is to say that if Bobby were to leave his wife and kids for his magical lady, the relationship would die. He would find out over time that his magical lady has just as many needs as his wife and the stressors of life are still there but now only worst. Now once again, this is just an example of how someone might cross over the line into stage 2. Some addicts will feel a "love" for their magical lady or mistress and don't want to hurt their families or their mistress. Other addicts have no emotional connection with the person they act out with and approach it almost like a drug deal or a means of conquest. In stage 2, the idol grows and demands more time and energy. It is no longer the "pocket idol" but has not yet become the 2 ton Buddha statue. Never the less the idol is like a black hole that sucks more and more life out of the addict.

Ill. 4

Sexual Addiction Relationship Line

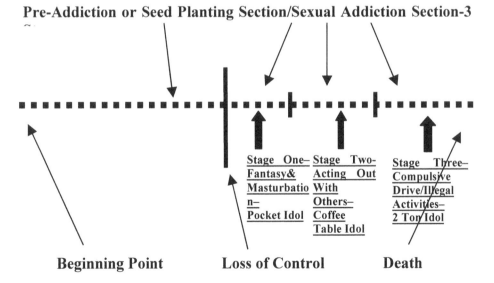

Pre-Addiction or Seed Planting Section/Sexual Addiction Section-3

| | Stage One– Fantasy& Masturbation– Pocket Idol | Stage Two– Acting Out With Others– Coffee Table Idol | Stage Three– Compulsive Drive/Illegal Activities– 2 Ton Idol |

Beginning Point   **Loss of Control**   **Death**

Stage 3- Illegal activities / Compulsive drive / The 2 ton Buddha Statue

If an addict crosses over into stage 3 he has now entered into an area where illegal activities exist and where the compulsive drive to act out becomes maddening. The addiction is now a 2 ton Buddha statue that is all consuming. The black hole has consumed almost every aspect of his life and the Beast is at its strongest point. Stage 3 addicts have received the most focus and attention through the years because they are generally forced into treatment or sent to jail. Because of this you have a contained population that you can study. In contrast, stage 1 addicts are harder to study because they may not get caught and they don't volunteer for research studies on sexual addiction. Just as in the 2 previous stages, the behaviors of the stage 3 addict will vary as well. This behavior will range from the use of prostitutes, child pornography to child molestation. Much earlier in the book I mentioned that sexual addiction is about death. This is a slow death that subtly occurs over time. By the time a man reaches stage 3, his emotions are deadened or totally desensitized. Spiritually he feels like God has abandoned him completely and his prayers do not reach higher than the ceiling. Mentally he cannot concentrate or focus and his creativity is gone. The only place he feels alive is in the addiction and even that is short- lived and he must push the envelope of risk taking further in order to obtain some type of high. Some behavior that began in stage 2 will continue into this stage but with more intensity and compulsivity. One of the big differences between stage 2 and 3 is the level of obsessive thinking a stage 3 addict will experience. With obsessive thinking an individual will grab a hold of a thought and they will not be able let go of that thought. For someone that obsesses about germs, they are unable to let go of the thought that their hands are dirty. No matter how much you reassure them their hands are clean, they cannot receive the message. The message "my hands are dirty" is super glued to their thoughts. The stage 3 addict is very similar in his thinking. His mind is controlled and consumed by obsessive sexual thoughts. These thoughts invade and consume his sleeping and waking hours. He cannot function at work or home because his concentration is consumed by the black hole of the addiction. Many stage 3 addicts will kill themselves to escape this maddening, obsessive and cyclical thinking. Stage 1 addicts will often read books that depict the behavior of stage 3 addicts and believe they are not addicts because they don't think about sex 24 hours a day. My response to that is, keep feeding and protecting the pocket idol and one day you will and that 2-ton statue will consume you.

Let's return to our story about Bobby. Bobby's affair with the single mom was eventually discovered. Bobby presented himself as a broken man before the leadership of the church and his wife. He is placed under church discipline and reassigned to be in charge of the greeters and the sound system. He is also required to attend counseling. Bobby did not act out in any way for several months and both he and his wife worked in martial counseling and attended a weekend marriage conference. Sounds like a good, sound, well intended plan of restoration. So, Bobby should stay free from his sexual sin and be able to walk in freedom the rest of his days. The problem is the addiction is not dead, it has just gone dormant. The heart of the beast or idol has not been dealt with. His behavior has been addressed and his job of being a husband has been fortified but not his core issues or his heart. God is always concerned with healing and cleansing our hearts. Bobby has been running from himself for a long time and until he deals with himself and his core issues, then the plant will grow back with reckless abandonment. Bobby now lives under a belief that he has been delivered and set free from his sexual sin. He believes his idol has been demolished. What will happen when the stressors of life return and he feels inadequate, a failure, rejected or abandoned? He looks into his tool box of life and finds no tools to deal with these events. There is one more piece to Bobby's story I need to include. Remember Bobby's father was his baseball coach and also minister. Well, his father was not just a minster; he was a very successful and well-loved minister. When Bobby was little his father was his hero and he aspired to be just like his Dad. As Bobby grew, he yearned and drove himself to obtain his father's approval. He always felt he fell short in each endeavor in his life. He couldn't wait to come home and tell his Dad the day he felt God's call to the ministry. His first week of seminary, he received a call from his mother that his father had died of a massive heart attack. You see at the core or heart of his addiction Bobby needed to know he measured up as a man and he had his father's approval and blessing. This need drove Bobby for many years. After his father's death, he put tremendous pressure upon himself in school to obtain the approval of his older seminary professors but never seemed to gain contentment.

He pushed himself to be the perfect husband, father and minister only to find disapproval and rejection. The only place he found where he measured up and didn't have to jump through hoops to get approval was in the fantasy world of the addiction.

If you would please refer to Psalm 51 and see if you can find any reference to David dealing with sexual sin. Even though this Psalm is David's process of restoration and healing from his sexual sin with Bathsheba, it is not mentioned. What David desires is for God to create in him a pure heart and a steadfast spirit. In other words, he wants to be cleansed in his inner most parts.

Psalm 51: 6-10 [6] *Behold, You desire truth in the inward parts, And in the hidden part You will make me to know wisdom.* [7] *Purge me with hyssop, and I shall be clean; Wash me, and I shall be whiter than snow.* [8] *Make me hear joy and gladness, That the bones You have broken may rejoice.* [9] *Hide Your face from my sins, and blot out all my iniquities.* [10] *Create in me a clean heart, O God, and renew a steadfast spirit within me.* (NKJV)

Deep in Bobby's heart is the need to know that he is unconditionally accepted, affirmed and validated. Until that void is addressed he will continue to struggle. He needs to learn to agree with God. In his head, he knows he is unconditionally loved by God but his heart does not agree with the Truth. You see there are barriers to Bobby's intimacy with God. With his repeated failures and disappointments in getting his needs met, he holds on to guilt and shame. The guilt and shame tell him it is his fault he is not getting his needs met and he just needs to try harder. This hidden core message of guilt and shame is a barrier to intimacy with God. Jesus bore the burden of our guilt and shame because we can't bear the burden. Unresolved guilt and shame coupled with frustration produces self-condemnation. Self-condemnation does not agree with God's grace, mercy and forgiveness.

2 Corinthians 10:4-5 [4] *For the weapons of our warfare are not carnal but mighty in God for pulling down strongholds,* [5] *casting down arguments and every high thing that exalts itself against the knowledge of God, bringing every thought into captivity to the obedience of Christ,* (NKJV)

In order for Bobby to demolish the stronghold of his addiction, he must also demolish arguments and lies that don't agree with Christ. In other words, the guilt, shame and anger in his heart have to be taken captive before God's Truth can cleanse him and restore him. When Bobby stopped his acting out, his full intention was to never go back. Most addicts will hit bottom several times in their life and each time will be committed to never return. The problem is when the addict stops medicating, he is right back where he started before the addiction began but even more miserable. The stress of life has intensified with the responsibilities of adult life. He still doesn't know how a Godly man deals with the stress of life. What he needs is tools and support that will prevent the reconstruction of his idol. He is still afraid to let others close because they may reject him or confirm that he is a failure. In Bobby's case, he is still looking for his father's approval and validation even though his father has been dead for several years.

This phase of non-acting out is similar to what a "dry drunk" might experience. An alcoholic may stop drinking for a period of time and try to "white knuckle" his way through recovery. During this period, the Beast is on life support and appears weak and non-threatening. He is miserable and so are the people around him. Bobby is not only miserable because he can't medicate, he is also miserable because he will never get the affirmation and approval he desires being in charge of the greeters and the sound system. Now he puts on the façade that he is grateful and content but on the inside, he feels trapped and frustrated. During this dormant, non-acting out, phase, Bobby tries what I refer to as "jumping ditches". In other words, he may trade addictions or use other escapes to deal with his pain. Some of these "ditches" may include alcohol, work, food or co-dependency. Some of his escapes may involve staying busy with activities, hobbies, TV, or exercise. These escapes are generally things which are socially acceptable but out of balance. Some escapes are budding addictions that, given the right stress, bloom into full blown addictions. Remember the guy on the Ed Sullivan Show who could keep several plates spinning on the top of individual sticks? That is the same picture as the "dry drunk" sex addict. He may have several addictions or escapes going on at the same time. He may continue in this state for quite a while as long as he receives some type of "drug" or reinforcement to continue. The work-a-holic receives the powerful drug of approval and affirmation. This becomes an even more powerful drug when they are a work-a-holic for the church. Bobby tries to find solace in affirmation from his job at the church but this affirmation "high" is only temporary and he continues to perform to obtain the next pat on the back. This affirmation "high" does not address his core need to be loved and affirmed without having to jump through hoops. He finds these performance "highs" do not work as well as the sexual addiction and he longs for the sanctuary of his fantasy world where there is no pressure to perform. He eventually returns to his addiction and reconstructing his idol, thinking that he will just go to the free sites on the internet and only once in a while when he needs to relieve some stress. Because he has been down this path before and the porn only frustrates him because it is not enough medication, he rapidly crosses over the line into Stage 3. Before he crosses over the line he goes through several one night stands and one on-going affair. He is caught again and this time his father's reputation cannot save his job and he is fired and forced to leave the ministry. His wife does not leave him by divorcing him but she does leave him emotionally. She immerses herself into her now teenage children and her career. Bobby is forced to take a job in sales where he has to travel quite a bit. Before long he notices the sites for the escort services during the lonely hours of his hotel room. The first time he acts out with a prostitute he feels shame but the second time he is totally desensitized. He buries the cost of his acting out in his business expense account. It becomes easier and easier to compartmentalize his out of town behavior. If he continues in this path, the addiction will kill every relationship in his life and eventually it will kill him.

The story of Bobby is not based upon an actual person but the composite picture of several. Each addict's story is different. The father's occupation could be anything from doctor to the town drunk. Some men are wounded intrusively and others non-intrusively. Some men find healing and restoration after self-disclosure early in Stage 1. While others hit several bottoms and never find healing and die alone with their addiction. It doesn't matter what the story is and how it plays out. It doesn't matter what an addict's plant of their addiction looks like. God is always most concerned with the condition of our hearts. If the heart of the addiction is not dealt with and the barriers to intimacy with God are not taken down then the plant of the addiction grows back.

In the south, we have plant that grows in the wild called kudzu. It grows so fast you can almost see it growing. This vine will consume everything in its path. You can cut and burn these vines repeatedly but it will grow back. It will even appear dead during the winter but it is only dormant. It is not until you dig up the tap root that you will be able to kill it. This is not an easy process because the tap root is covered with years of vine growth and it often penetrates very deep into the soil. The same thing is true of sexual addiction. The leaves and vines of the kudzu represent the sinful behavior that is produced. The addict can do some extreme things to keep the vines from growing back. Stopping the sinful behavior of the addiction is paramount to the recovery process we will address in the next chapter. However, if you just deal with the behavior of the addiction and stop there then the plant will grow back. In some point of the healing and recovery process the Christian sex addict needs to deal with the tap root or the core issues of his addiction. Before we close this chapter, let me remind you our discussion is centered on how this addiction affects Christian men. Non-Christian sex addicts do not always have core issues to address. In other words, sinners sin because it is what they are supposed to do and they enjoy their sin. They do not have the conviction of the Holy Spirit and only a very limited view of what healthy intimacy with others looks like.

Chapter 4

One Man's Journey to Freedom

"Growing up in the buckle of the Bible Belt was a gift whose importance I cannot overstate. Most African American families like mine were church-going. My mother was a Sunday school teacher. My step-father attended regularly, and my biological father directed the choir at his respective house of prayer. It allowed me to have the opportunity to learn about Jesus at an early age. It gave me the chance to be around worship, praise, and fiery, Baptist preaching. During after-church suppers of fried chicken, chitlins, yams, and greens, I would hear older family members exclaim, "Didn't Rev. preach today?"

"Sho' 'nuf did, child!"

"The Holy Ghost showed up and showed out!" another would chime in.

As I recall those memories, there are others that are in the corner of my mind that are not so pleasant. Many of these same people who were talking about how good the Lord was were also NOT talking about some very serious issues that proved to be a cancer in our family. It began to infect me and manifest itself in my life by the time I was only a four-year old.

Four teenaged female family members began to experiment with me sexually when I began my kindergarten year. I had no idea of what was going on, or even why it was happening. I couldn't understand it at that time, but I was sucked into a world of misery and mayhem that would not let me go for many, many years. I would remain a prisoner of myself and the dark forces that would attempt to control my every action. And the worst part of it was that I liked it somewhere deep inside my twisted little mind.

On the tablet of my being different people were etching a story for me whose theme was not one I would have chosen. As the abuse continued, I considered it a "normal" part of my existence; something I even began to look forward to. In addition to the family members, there was a young 5th grade substitute teacher who used to bring select boys to the restroom for "counseling." To me it was nothing new, more of the same. By that time, I thought it was the way things were supposed to be.

After my family moved, the abuse from the family members stopped, but I didn't have to wait long for the deviant and devilish to present itself to me. By that time my biological father began to show renewed interest in me. He happened to have adult magazines and pornographic videos in plain sight. The dirty magazines were displayed on the coffee table along with "Ebony," "Sports Illustrated," and "Esquire." The pornographic movies were shelved right beside "48 Hours," "Star Wars III," and "Ghost Busters." Why he thought that was acceptable, I'll never know. Therefore, when I went to spend the occasional week with him during the summer months, I had ready access to as much filth as I wanted. Around the age of 13, my father gave me "the talk" by presenting me with a box of condoms and asking if I knew how to use them. I told him I did. He advised if I needed more to just ask. The devil was tightening his grip.

Beyond that, my step-father bought a satellite dish, much to my delight. It was my job to find the adult channels for him and mark them on the dish crank with special notches so that he'd know where they were if I wasn't at home to find them for him. So many nights as he and my mother watched the porn in their bedroom in the back of the house, I'd be watching the same movie in the front of the house while munching chips and sipping soda. I was in a hole that knew no bottom. I kept falling deeper and deeper.

Throughout high school and college, I still chased girls and watched porn in spite of giving my life to Christ in the 10th grade. I had absolutely no idea of what a healthy relationship was supposed to look like. I had not seen anyone walk the word as a dedicated believer. All of the respected church folk I knew used me to run porn between them and my step-father. I thought that was all there was to being a Christian; going to church, that is. I knew how to live the life of the religious. I knew it well. What I didn't know was how to have a relationship with Jesus Christ.

It wasn't until I began to actually read the bible for myself and study the scripture that the Holy Spirit began to convict me severely about my way of life during my college years. I began to see how the way that I was living was diametrically opposed to the life that Christ prescribed. As strong as my desire was to follow Christ and let him lead, my flesh had reigned longer and did not want to die.

I continued wrestling with this conundrum until I finally met the woman of my dreams. I thought to myself: This is just the ticket. I just need to get married. Once I'm married, then I'll have all the sex I want available all the time. And I really love her, so it'll be different. How tragic that I'd reduced my wife to ready pleasure for my personal needs. Furthermore, I made her responsible for fixing something that she didn't break. That was too much of a burden to place on an unknowing victim: my wife. It was unfair that she became the surrogate of my sin. It was a dangerous proposition because when sin is fully conceived, it brings death.

Of course, the predictable happened. I didn't remain faithful, and as a result I almost lost my wife and children. But because God is merciful, and my wife was forgiving, I got another chance. Subsequently, as a condition of staying with me my wife demanded that I get counseling and attend a men's group for men with my type of problem... sex addiction. Sex addiction? Yep. I was a bona fide sex addict. I didn't learn that until Jonathan Jones told me what ailment I was suffering from. I figured I'd go to the meetings for about 3 or 4 months before going back to "regular life." I figured because I was sorry and repentant that I'd be okay in no time. It's four years later, and I'm still attending those meetings.

They keep my sin before me, which helps me keep things in perspective. What things? Well, first that I no longer have to carry the guilt and shame of my past. Secondly, I can forgive those who've damaged me in the past because of the forgiveness God has given me, no longer blaming anyone for my actions. Finally, those meetings keep me accountable to a group of men who are full of grace; men who walk the walk I walk with compassion and care.

Everyone's relationship with their sexual sin is different. Learning how to cope with denying myself was akin to a dope fiend going through withdrawal. I literally had to detoxify myself of all the mess in my life. Coming to the realization that my addiction wasn't about what it was about made everything much clearer, also. Setting boundaries and limiting opportunities for slip-ups became a priority as I sought to walk as a true kingdom man. Clint Eastwood once remarked in one of his "Dirty Harry" movies, "A man's gotta know his limitation." That's sage advice.

I'm not yet at the end of my journey, because it's a work in progress. But I'm well on my way. Being free is a good thing! Someone once said that the two greatest days in your life was the day you were born, and the day you realize what you were born for. I was born to be free to glorify God and fulfill my calling as His child! Are you free? Where are you on your journey? If you don't know, I can help point you in the right direction."

The Healing / Recovery Process

Before we start this chapter, let me reiterate something I said in the introduction. This is not a self-help book or manual. You cannot change, heal or fix yourself. I say that knowing that right now some of you are in the pursuit of trying to get your "why" questions answered. You believe that if you can get your "why" questions answered then you can bring order to the chaos that is caused by your own addiction or a loved one's addiction. I believe that answering our "why" questions are not anywhere on God's list of priorities for us.

First of all, God does not owe us an answer to our questions. Secondly, our faith does its most growth in God's unanswered "why" questions. Job asked God the "why" question numerous times but when God spoke he did not answer any of his questions. Instead what Job received was being humbled and having a closer walk with God.

Recovery from sexual addiction is a hard and difficult journey that can become intensely painful at times. If you are willing to let God crush you and purge you, then you are ready to begin. If you are looking for a quick fix and a painless journey then I am sorry to say you are not ready to be healed.

John 5: 3-6 *³ In these lay a great multitude of sick people, blind, lame, paralyzed, waiting for the moving of the water. ⁴ For an angel went down at a certain time into the pool and stirred up the water; then whoever stepped in first, after the stirring of the water, was made well of whatever disease he had. ⁵ Now a certain man was there who had an infirmity thirty-eight years. ⁶ When Jesus saw him lying there, and knew that he already had been in that condition a long time, He said to him, "Do you want to be made well?"* (NKJV)

Jesus, in John chapter 5, met a paralyzed man who for 38 years had been lying by the pool of Bethesda. The legend of the pool centered upon the story that angels would enter the water and stir the pool. If someone were to enter the pool while the water was still moving they could be healed of their infirmity. This man had placed his faith in what most people believe was a fairy tale for 38 years. Jesus asked this man a very strange question. He asked "Do you want to be healed?" instead of answering yes or no, he gave an explanation as to why his healing or recovery had not worked. If you ask a broken Christian sex addict the same question he might say, "Yes, of course I do, look at all I've done through the years to be healed." My follow up question is "What do you want to be healed of?" Most addicts want to be healed of the pain and hurt the addiction has and is causing them and others. Some want to be delivered from their sexually inappropriate behavior. There is nothing wrong with wanting relief from pain and stopping sinful behavior. Maybe, however, God wants to heal the addict of something even deeper and more important to him. God is always concerned with changing people at their core or heart. What he wants to heal, change and restore is the wounded spirit and he wants to fill those core needs with his pure and perfect love. In order to have a human spirit healed, restored, changed and filled, we have to be willing to let God crush and break our human spirits. To allow him to crush our prideful, arrogant, narcissistic, and self-directed human spirit. Without the broken and contrite spirit the steps to healing will fall short, and relapse into sexual sin is inevitable. I understand that some of you reading this are the ones struggling with sexual sin and others reading this are in relationship with the struggler. As we go through each step I will attempt to address both viewpoints.

Before we begin the process of identifying the steps to recovery, I first need to point out the most important element of all. That element is prayer. Prayer should be interwoven into all of these steps. You should not proceed into any area without covering it in prayer. This will be especially true the closer we get to the issues at the core or the heart of the addiction. If you are at a point in your journey you believe you can't pray then follow this old advice, "if you can't pray, pray until you can". Just pray. God will listen. He will hear your cry and direct your steps. If you are the loved one of someone in denial and rebellion regarding their sexual sin then surrender them in prayer to their heavenly Father. This is not giving up. It is giving over something you have no control over to the someone who does. You may have to do this every day and rest in the fact your love has limits but His does not and His can bring about brokenness and change.

Step 1- Brokenness

Psalm 51: 17 *The sacrifices of God are a broken spirit, A broken and a contrite heart— These, O God, You will not despise.* (NKJV)

The first step in healing has already been mentioned and that is brokenness. I worked in a psychiatric hospital for many years. In this hospital was a locked unit for individuals who were a danger to themselves or others. Many times, when I would meet a new client for the first time on this unit they would say "I give up, I quit, I can't go on." Often my response to this statement would be "Good, now are you ready to let God take full control of your life?" I was not trying to be mean spirited. I wanted to know if they really were at a place of brokenness and surrender. Until the addict reaches his point of nothingness and completely surrenders to God then he will continue to think he is in control. When the addict is at this place of "God I give up, I quit, I can't fix myself" then he is ready for healing or recovery to begin. This is a common question, "How can I tell if my husband is really broken? Because he is a master manipulator and he has fooled everybody for years." What she is asking is how she can tell if what she is seeing is a burnt offering or a genuine broken and contrite spirit. In other words, is this just show-n-tell and manipulating or the real deal. There are 2 ways to know if this is real brokenness. The first sign that he is really broken is when he is willing to do whatever it takes to be healed. That means he is the one finding a counselor, support group, and developing a support system. He does not let embarrassment of others finding out about his sin stop him. He is putting the same level of energy into getting well that he did into getting sick. The second way to know if his brokenness is real is more long term and that is to watch his fruit or behavior. On a long-term basis is he producing real fruit of the spirit and not fake fruit. An old adage to remember during this time is "Listen to the words but trust the behavior." This does not mean that the recovering addict has to be perfect and will never make a mistake. This means that the recovering addict is in a repetitive pattern of pursuing righteousness and purity. Later on, we will discuss how others can aid the recovering addict in his healing process. It never ceases to amaze me when I discover what some addict's bottoms are and how much they have to lose before they realize what they are doing is not working. I learned a long time ago, people will keep doing what they are doing until it cost them enough or it is not working. What amazes me even more is a Christian addict does not have to lose everything. When we bring our sin before our Holy, Pure and Righteous God then it will bring us to that point of brokenness, where the healing begins. The pain of brokenness does not produce true and longstanding change.

God allows pain to get our attention and informs us what we are doing is not working and we are out of his will. Brokenness informs us that we are powerless on our own and we need to surrender the control of our lives completely to Him. From brokenness, we eventually move into humility and walking out a life that is dependent upon Him. Brokenness is the beginning of recovery and not the end.

Step 2- Honesty

Ephesians 6:14 *Stand therefore, having girded your waist with truth, having put on the breastplate of righteousness*, (NKJV)

The second step is honesty. The sex addict has to commit to total and complete honesty in order to be healed. In Ephesians 6:14, the first piece of the spiritual armor is the Belt of Truth. Without the Belt of Truth then the Breastplate of Righteous is useless because it hooks to the belt. Without an effective breastplate then the heart is exposed. The Sword of Truth or God's word is connected to the Belt of Truth as well. Without the Belt of Truth, you have an ineffective warrior who is easily defeated. Without a commitment to complete honesty then the addict cannot receive complete restoration and forgiveness. I would like for you to picture forgiveness and restoration abiding in a distant town or city. The addict lives in the city of despair and hopelessness. Honesty is the road that takes him from that place so he too can abide in the place of true forgiveness and restoration. He will need to practice honesty with discernment. Finding Godly counsel in developing this discernment will be needed.

Let's return to our story of Bobby. After Bobby's affair is discovered he has a broken and contrite spirit, but he is not totally honest. He is only honest about what he has been caught doing. Because of his shame and guilt, he is not honest about his extensive use of porn. He is not honest about his feelings of rejection and failure regarding his marriage and his father. Without complete honesty, the effects of the brokenness will soon fade away. God compares us to sheep and sheep have a very short term memory. With a short-term memory and having little ability to deal with pain, the addict returns to his idol. Brokenness and honesty must go hand in hand. There is an old adage which says "You are just as sick as your secrets." Honesty breaks the power these secrets have upon your life.

Step 3- Getting Sober

Once brokenness and honesty are established as the corner stones for recovery then the third step can begin. The third step is dealing with the sinful behavior of the addict or getting sober from their sexual idolatry. This may sound like I am contradicting myself because I spent so much time talking about dealing with the core issues. You cannot deal with the core issues while you are still medicating them. It is like trying to reason with someone that is drunk. It is a waste of time.

As we enter into this step, let me say that the addict can't do this by himself. The addict must have accountability with other Godly men. Throughout the book, I will be referring to these men as "men of grace."

John 1: 14 *And the Word became flesh and dwelt among us, and we beheld His glory, the glory as of the only begotten of the Father, full of grace and truth.* (NKJV)

When the Word, Jesus, came into the world he brought with him the union of grace and truth and he never uncoupled those two and always kept them in perfect balance. Men of grace are accountability and support partners who strive for that balance. In other words, they will always speak and rely upon His Truth but also point you toward the sufficiency of His Grace. They will provide accountability and they will also meet needs.

One way to define accountability is providing external discipline in an area where the addict lacks internal discipline. To expect an addict to immediately have internal discipline regarding his thoughts is setting him up to fail. For non-addicts reading this, it may appear that based upon the cost of their addiction and the power of God working in their lives then the addict should forsake this sinful lifestyle immediately. Let me try to explain why this can be difficult. During our teenage years, we should be practicing saying "no" to our wants and desires more than we say "yes" to them. This promotes the growth of self-denial as well as strengthening our spiritual muscles by saying "no" to what I want and "yes" to what God's will is for me. In most cases, the developing sex addict has never practicing saying no to wants and desires regarding sexual temptation. Therefore, there is no resistance or practice at saying "no" to his fleshly desires. He needs other men to challenge and encourage him to work the "muscles" of spiritual resistance.

Let me stress here that accountability for a male sex addict needs to come from other males. The addict's wife does not need to be his primary accountability partner in his sexual addiction recovery. This does not take away from the addict's second step of honesty regarding his wife.

Sexual addicts are going to have "mental slips" during their recovery. Our brains are like computers that don't forget anything especially intense things such as sexual stimulation. Sometimes in the addict's recovery process the addict's mind will open an old sexual file and reminisce about that behavior. That can appear in the addict's mind like a pop-up on a computer screen. The addict didn't ask to see the file, it just popped-up because he has trained his brain to store this information for many years. Sometimes the addict views an attractive woman for 1 second, turns away, but his thoughts slip into sexually objectifying her image. These are just a couple of examples of mental slips and most addicts will experience these even when they are working their hardest in recovery. We will address in a later chapter some of the steps in dealing slip, slides and falls. If the addict tells his wife every time he has a mental slip, he will drive her crazy. "Oh, by the way, Honey while I was at the store getting the milk, I saw an attractive woman, was able to turn away, pray and avoid lustful thoughts toward her. Thanks for letting me share. What's for supper?" After a while of doing this, the wife will wear down because she doesn't know what to do with this information. She just wants to feel emotionally and spiritually safe in her relationship with her husband. When, not if, the addict has a mental slip he must assault it by bringing it into truth and reality. When a child catches on fire you teach them to stop, drop and roll. Hopefully, you teach a child this before they catch fire and hopefully never have to use this information. The first thing an addict does when he has a mental slip is stop, drop and pray. The prayer may sound like this, "God, I just got an image of that lady in the milk section that I don't need or want. So, God will you please cleanse my thoughts of this impurity." This prayer is done live and in color on the spot. They do not need to maximize this event nor do they need to minimize it. If this assault upon this image is delayed then the next step may be a slide and not a slip. It is easier to correct a slip rather than a slide. The addict needs to view this slip as an opportunity to bring his thoughts into obedience and the process of renewing his mind. Sometimes, even after the addict has prayed repeatedly, the image is still in his brain. If this occurs then the addict needs to do a "fire drill". Some of the men in the addict's accountability system will to be "firemen" and some will not. The addict needs a group of men or "firemen" he can call when he has a mental slip that won't stop or when there is an emergency. What happens is the addict is slipping into the compartmentalized relationship of the addiction for just a moment because he hasn't yet developed internal discipline or spiritual "muscle" strength over his thought life. Because women do not compartmentalize as men do, the wife is unable to understand or relate. Over time, if the addict's only accountability is his wife, she will feel used and frustrated because she can't understand why he just can't stop. The addict will sense his wife's frustration and he interprets this as a message of failure and rejection. He will stop confiding in his wife regarding his slips because he doesn't want to be seen as a failure to his wife and has no clue of how a Godly man deals with failure. Thus, he becomes dishonest and violates step 2 of the recovery process and takes one step toward a slide and relapse. There are other reasons why men need accountability from men but we will address those later.

In the beginning of his healing or recovery process he needs other men with whom he can be totally honest and will hold him accountable regarding his sexual thoughts and behavior. If I am a sex addict's primary accountability person, I will often say to them; "If I tell you to stand on your head and stack B-B's wearing boxing gloves, I want you to do it. Because your very best thinking got you sitting here with me." At first glance this may sound cruel and shaming, but it is not. The addict, early in his recovery, needs to understand that his thoughts have become distorted and in some cases damaged by this addiction. His thoughts need to go through a period of detoxification and purification. The addict needs one primary accountability partner who will hold his feet to the fire and who knows the whole story. In some recovery circles this person is known as a sponsor or a mentor. This person can be a pastor, counselor, friend or part of an established support group. We will address more specific ways to set up accountability with men of grace and addressing slip, slides and falls in a later chapter.

Some 12 Step groups have been using sponsors for years and have clearly defined guidelines for this responsibility. Along with this primary accountability partner it is helpful and beneficial for the addict to attend sexual addiction support or recovery groups. In some areas of the country these groups can be easier to find than others. In areas where there are very few options for support groups then the addict may have to, with the aid of his pastor or counselor, start his own group. If there are support group options in the area, then he must determine if the group is a good fit for his needs and doesn't violate scripture in what is being taught. In other words, finding a good healthy group that meets the addict's needs, will take some time.

In step 3, the addict would also benefit from counseling or therapy. Let me stress something right away. The addict, if married, does not need intensive marital counseling in the beginning of his recovery. In the beginning, the addict and his wife both need individual counseling and healing. If you put a sex addict into marital therapy too soon it will trigger his core fears of failure, abandonment and rejection and all his defense mechanisms or walls will go up. If done too soon, the addict goes into marriage counseling "looking good", managing his image and the wife looks out of control. The wife comes away feeling unheard and the addict feels validated that he really doesn't have a problem. This healing process is about revival and revival always starts with the individual. In order for there to be healing in the marriage, each person needs their own revival process. The agent of change is the Holy Spirit. Sometimes God can use us to help change others but first I need to let God change me through the power of His Holy Spirit. Sometimes this revival begins with the spouse of the addict and other times with the addict. When we are cleansed and revived then we can be a conduit for God's Living Water to flow through us to those around us. It is His Love or Living Water that changes people's hearts and not our human love.

Finding an individual therapist or counselor can be tricky and time consuming but well worth the effort. The perfect situation would be to find one that is trained in dealing with sexual addiction from a Christian perspective and foundation. Look in the Yellow Pages, Christian publications, get a referral from a friend, and call national ministries that provide referral services or call local churches to see who they refer to for this issue. Perfect Hope Ministries (www.perfecthope.org) would be glad to assist you in this process and discuss our workshop options. Give us a call at 901-430-3412 or email me at perfecthope.org@gmail.com. Once you have some names, call and interview them to make sure they are a good fit for you. If you are the love one of a sex addict please do not do the calling, interviewing and scheduling for the addict. Remember if they are really broken, then they will be willing to do whatever it takes to be healed and that includes making phone calls. Have a set of questions prepared to ask such as, "How do you incorporate scripture and prayer into your counseling? Do you have someone I could call as a reference? How long have you been counseling and how many sexual addicts have you counseled?" If they are unwilling to be interviewed by phone then cross them off your list. Be patient, however, because they may be very busy and it could take some time for them to get back to you. This therapist will also play a key part in dealing with the core issues and/or past wounds. The addict may also have multiple addictions, co-addictions and/or secondary addictions. Being assessed by a trained addiction therapist can help in keeping the addict from "jumping ditches". A vital part of recovery is developing an effective battle plan. Your counselor can help develop an individual plan that fits your unique relationship with your sexual sin. This should involve understanding your addiction cycle, sexual triggers, effective spiritual warfare and utilizing your accountability partners in this fight.

Let's do a brief review before we go to Step 4. The addict needs to be at a point of brokenness and committed to being honest. From this place of brokenness comes the willingness to do whatever it takes to be healed. Complete honesty is paramount because part of breaking the bondage of addiction and secrets is bringing the light of truth into the darkness. The addict needs to be completely honest with himself, God and others. Partial honesty will result in him "stashing" away past shameful events and will limit him experiencing God's complete forgiveness and restoration. With brokenness and honesty in union, the addict is now ready for Step 3. The addict cannot find sobriety or healing by trying to do this alone. He needs the support and accountability of Godly men. Finding the right support group and individual counselor will take time but it can be essential for the recovery process. Recovery is not for the faint of heart and it is not a sprint but more like a marathon race. Recovery is also not an event, it is a process and it takes time and sacrifice but it is worth it.

Step 4 – Stabilizing Disorders

Step 4 involves assessing and treating the addict's physical, emotional and psychiatric disorders or conditions. Some addicts may not experience any disorders related to their addiction while others have disorders that are their most pervasive or presenting issue. In either case the addict will need a thorough assessment. The therapist that was defined in Step 3 can assist in determining if these disorders are in place by doing a thorough assessment or referring to someone who can. If the addict is not stable or healthy in the physical, emotional, or psychiatric areas then it will be difficult and sometimes hazardous for them to continue in the healing process. Let's take some time to look at each area.

Regarding the physical care of his body, most addicts do poorly in attending to this area. For some they have not had a complete physical in several years. Stage 2 and 3 addicts need to get a physical as well being tested for STD's. A note to the wives of Stage 2 and 3 addicts: If you have recently discovered your husband has had sexual contact or relations with someone else, stop having sex with him. You need to go to your doctor and be tested and follow his/her advice. Having sex with your husband will not stop him from acting out with others and you are putting yourself at risk. If you are married to a Stage 1, 2, or 3 sex addict and you are 100 percent sure there is no chance for disease, then you still need to take a sexual fast. His brain, in the early stages needs time to detox and heal. Chemically speaking, his brain does not know whether he is having sex with you or his addiction. Finding a Christian addiction counselor will help guide both of you through this process.

If during the physical assessment there is a discovered area of concern then these areas need to be stabilized before the recovering addict can continue in his recovery. For example, if a physical exam indicates there is hyper-tension then it may not be safe to continue until this is stabilized through a doctor's care. There are also certain physical conditions that can affect our moods and emotions. A word of caution: addicts are always looking for people and things to blame and take the focus away from their "idol". Finding "something wrong" with them physically can become a reason or excuse to stop the healing/recovery process.

The next area which may need assessing is the psychiatric and emotional area. I encourage people to seek out doctors who are specialized in their area of concern. It may be convenient and less costly to let your general practitioner assess you both physically and psychiatrically but the second area will be out of his specialty. It would be most beneficial to find a Christian Psychiatrist that is also trained in the area of addictions. If this is not possible then we refer back to the complete honesty rule because an addict can produce false symptoms. Without the whole story the doctor may attempt to treat the symptoms. There are varying opinions and feelings regarding the use of psychotropic medications. Some believe the use of medication will diminish what God is trying to do in their lives and shows a lack of faith. Others may believe it is foolish to suffer when there is reliable help available. Maybe the truth lies somewhere in the middle of both of these opinions. Maybe medication, when appropriate, can be an aid and assist the healing process and the right usage will not result in over medicating or numbing of emotions. Several years ago, I had someone apply for a workshop and during the interview it became evident he was confused and unable to stay focused during our conversation. He also mentioned thoughts of wanting to die. I referred him to a psychiatrist for an assessment. He was diagnosed with a Bipolar illness, placed on medication and over time found relief from this condition that had plagued him for years. He eventually was stable enough to attend a workshop and because of his stabilization was able to concentrate and focus upon the information provided. Another area of concern can appear during the physical or the psychiatric evaluation and that is eating disorders. It is not uncommon for sex addicts to struggle with some type of eating disorder. This disorder can be part of the "ditch jumping" or a co-addiction issue. If an addict is unable to use his sexual addiction to medicate he may turn to food as a source of comfort.

During this stage, the triage approach to dealing with these disorders will be important. This approach will identify what area presents the greatest concern. In some cases, the addict's disorder will need to be addressed first. In other cases, the disorders may be minimal, only requires monitoring or may not exist. Let me stress this again. Not every sexual addict has a disorder while some have their disorders immerge after months or years of sobriety. Do not try to diagnosis this on your own, through Google searches or by comparing your recovery to someone else's. You will need a professional assessment and diagnosis if pervasive symptoms manifest themselves.

"That can't be right! This clock must be broken. There is no way it is that late. I'm forgetting something. I'm supposed to be somewhere. Oh, no! This is Saturday. Todd's first soccer game is today. It's already over. I promised him I would be there. What kind

of jerk am I? My Dad never came to anything I was in. I am just like him. No, I am worst. I'm not a drunk. I don't have any excuses.

"What am I going to do? I only set down to check some emails and that was 3 hours ago. How did I get on these sites? How many images have I seen? My head hurts. I have got to think. My wife said she'd leave me if I looked at porn again. Where did the time go? That has been happening a lot lately. It's the stress at work. I need to go see my doctor maybe he can give me something to get my focus back. What am I going to tell my wife and son? I know. I will tell them a church member had a crisis. She knows better than to ask who it was. Todd will understand. After all, a pastor's job is 24/7. I won't be back here again. This is crazy. If anyone found out, I'd lose my church and never preach again. It doesn't matter because I won't be doing this again. I said that last time. This time is different."

Robert

Step 6 – Spiritual Assessment

You may find it odd I placed the spiritual assessment in step 6 and not in the very beginning. You may be asking "why did you not address the addict's salvation and his relationship with Christ earlier? Isn't it a waste of time to for this person to become sober and free from sexual sin and spend eternity in Hell? Don't we know who the believers are by the fruit they produce? Well, look at the fruit this addict has produced. Does that look like the fruit of someone who is saved?" These are all very good questions and I will attempt to address the rationale behind the placement of this assessment here.

First of all, the spiritual assessment does not have to come in at this point of recovery. It may come much earlier. It needs to be addressed no later than this point. If the addict is a non-Christian then the steps that follow will not apply to him and it will be an act of frustration for the addict and his support system. If it is very clear the addict is not a Christian at this juncture and wants no part of the plan of salvation then he will need to be referred to a secular counselor and support network. We want everyone to come to know the Lord and no one would perish. The truth is more people reject His gift than receive it. Those who reject it still deserve to have a sober and healthy life. Several years ago, I was about to begin a workshop with a young man struggling with sexual addiction. I stated, "Let's pray before we begin." His immediate response was, "Hold on just a minute, I'm not very religious, my wife is the religious one and wanted me to see a Christian." After a very long discussion, he made it very clear that he was not a Christian and did not want to be pressured into becoming one. I could not make this young man, who was by the way in the military and leaving to go into combat as soon as we finished our time together, accept the gift Christ freely offered him. I needed to respect him and afford him grace even knowing he was about to enter harm's way. He still needed tools to be sober and healthy. I had done secular addiction counseling in the past and gave him some practical tools he might be able to use. As he began to trust me I would attempt to draw the topic back to Jesus and he would allow it because he knew I respected him. I would like to say that he accepted Christ before he left but he did not. My hope and prayer is seeds were planted and God used someone else to water. Maybe the prayers and example of a Godly wife led him the rest of the way. I bring this example up to say if you are clearly dealing with a non-believer and you are in the counseling or pastoral role and you do not have what this person needs, then refer to someone who does.

There is an old saying, "Your behavior is speaking so loudly that I can't see who you are." When an addict's compartmentalized addictive behavior comes into the light, it is often shocking and sometimes over whelming because those around the addict have only been allowed to see the image and facade he managed to hide behind. When this behavior is exposed it is easy to not be able to see beyond this behavior and assume he can't be a Christian and have done all these egregious acts. We may define the addict by this newly discovered behavior. I have known numerous Christian sex addicts who have been "saved" dozens of times but only to have the kudzu vine of their addiction grow back. I bring this issue up to say, "don't assume anything and timing that is prompted and directed by the Holy Spirit is paramount." Don't assume someone is not saved based solely upon a brief review of their behavior. This assumption may not be accurate. If you are in the counseling role with the sex addict then you need to be sensitive to the direction of the Holy Spirit. A large number of sex addicts also struggle with people pleasing. If they are presented with the plan of salvation, they may give you the "right answer" as a way of making everything okay and everyone alright with them. They will say the right words out of pleasing man and not pleasing God. Another reason why timing is so important in assessing the addict's salvation status is based upon the addict's mind set. If you are dealing with a sex addict who also has an addictive personality then he may view salvation as a quick fix or another "high" that will make him feel better. The addictive mind set is to always look for something to make you feel better instantly, avoid all pain, seek anything that will be a medicate or escape from your pain. When I was a teenager the poplar phrase was "get high on Jesus". The addict may perceive salvation as a way that he can "get high on Jesus" and avoid dealing with any of the pain his addiction has caused because his sins are now "under the Blood" and no one can bring them up or hold him accountable. Sexual addicts who are in fact saved may confess to not being saved in an attempt to avoid the pain involved and please others at the same time.

This step can become very complicated as well as a very sensitive subject. I believe the challenge for the church today is not only to get people saved but also to know how to minister to the wounded who are already in our family of God. That includes the ones that are wounded by their own selfish rebellion. If we are not careful the church in America will become one which presents salvation as a list checking event that is void of true relationship with Christ and the body of believers. Testimonies have become what I call "cocaine stories" that start with "Before I knew the Lord I did... (fill in the blank) ...the Lord saved me and I ain't done... (fill in the blank) ... since. Praise the Lord!" When was the last time you heard a testimony that said "I came to know the Lord at an early

up in a Christian home, have been employed by the chur

the mission field, seen God's miracles first hand but I rebelled anyway." In other words, I knew better and rebelled in spite of that knowledge <u>but</u> God's love and was still greater than all my sin. His Grace was more than sufficient to cover all my sins." I call these "testimony Part 2". If you are in the counseling role or in relationship with the sexual addict, please don't be too hasty to judge the condition of the addict's salvation upon his behavior. Please do not offer salvation as a quick fix to the addict's problems and pain. Please do rely upon the prompting of the Holy Spirit and sit down and listen to the addict. God will reveal to you the condition of the addict's heart over time. If you are the pastor or counselor who is assessing the spiritual condition of the addict then you need to develop a list of open ended questions which allows them to talk. The questions/requests may sound something like this; "Tell me about your relationship with God and your experience with religion. When did you feel closest to God and when did you feel far away from him? Have you ever experienced intimacy with God? Tell me about your understanding of salvation." Give yourself plenty of time for this assessment. You can give written assignments prior to your meeting which may help with your assessment. You can ask the addict to write out their spiritual story or time line. Once again, the most important thing is to listen and allow God's timing to occur. If you will allow steps 1 and 2 of brokenness and honesty to occur, then the Holy Spirit will do the work of conviction. Please understand this section may be the most time consuming but also the most important. Once again prayer is paramount before and during this step.

"It is strange the thoughts that go through your head when your world has just been destroyed. Maybe it's your mind's way of coping because reality is too much to handle. I spent an entire life creating a fantasy world and now reality has demolished its well protected boundaries.

I always liked watching those cop shows and wondered how a criminal could be so stupid. Couldn't they tell that was a cop offering them the drugs or sex? Now who's the stupid criminal? Look in his rear-view mirror. That guy's reflection staring back at you through the mess wire screen, that's you stupid. That driver's license he has in his hand is yours. The information he is speaking into the mic on his shoulder is your name, address, and driver's license number. The wrists that those handcuffs are biting into are yours.

You can't be here. You're too smart. You've always been able to talk your way out of things. Entrapment that's what it was. I never gave him money. What will my wife and kids say? They will never let me see the grand kids again.

What did he say? "Yes officer, I'm Dr. Smith." I am going to lose everything. Wife, family, career, reputation: everything. What was the pastor's sermon about? He said something about grace being able to cover a multitude of sins. How did I get here? None of this makes sense. Why and how could I trade in everything for an orgasm with a total stranger? What will happen next? I guess I will find out soon enough. The officer says we're going to the station for processing. I wish he would stop calling me Doc. How did I get here?" *Allan*

Chapter 5

"I remember the first nude pictures I ever saw. I remember ever thing about that day. I remember my father's disappointment that I hadn't made the cut for the ball team. Oh, he didn't say anything but I can still see that look of disappointment in his eyes. I knew that look very well. I didn't just see it from him. My mom had the look too. Her look always came when I failed at school or forgot to do something she had asked. I saw it with my friends when I made the last out in kick ball. I saw it from my grandfather when I couldn't drive a nail straight. Boy, did I know "the look" of disappointment. I saw something different that day out in the woods. We were looking for a place to build a new fort. It's important for 12-year-old boys to have a fort that they can call their own. The old fort had been overrun by some new "cool" kids and us un-cool kids were branching out on our own. We were in a new part of the woods that we had never ventured into. We came upon a site with an old campfire and various discards and cast away items of life. There were empty beer cans, an old mattress, various rags of previously worn clothes, and old magazines. I was the first to come across "the magazines". As I look back upon that moment, I realize what grabbed me first were her eyes. Her eyes were warm, caring and most of all accepting. In less than an instant, I took in the entirety of the picture and her lack of clothing. Here I am over 30 years later and I can still see that picture.

I know now that I tried to recreate that experience thousands of times through the years. Whenever I felt, perceived or experienced "the look" of disappointment, I would escape into fantasy world of

102

acceptance. I even believed that God looked at me with constant disappointment because I could never please him. There was never disappointment in the eyes of the magical ladies of porn, strippers, or prostitutes. Only looks of acceptance.

I've been clean from sexual idolatry for several years now. I still need support and accountability because I know how quickly I can return to my vomit. I don't miss the shame and guilt. In a weird way, you can say I'm addicted to pursuing purity. I relate to that Pinocchio character. I'm a real boy/man now and being alive feels really good.

I am still learning to deal with reality. Reality involves conflict, disappointment and rejection. Reality also involves restoration, reconciliation, mercy, grace, forgiveness and love. I choose reality, by the Grace of God, each day."

Charles

Barriers, Thieves and Compulsions
Taking Down the Walls

Before we fully jump into the meat of this chapter, I need to point out a few things first. This area can be the most frustrating part of the addict's recovery. At this point in recovery the addict may be feeling better because he may have a few months of sobriety under his belt and the people around him are encouraged by his progress. I did a workshop with a recovering sex addict several years ago who had over 6 years of sobriety from his sexual sin. He was now ready to begin his venture into his core issues, heart of the Beast and the tap root of his addiction. This section of recovery can be very painful and the addict may become frustrated with the process because he thought he was past the pain of recovery. It is through this next part of recovery he begins to grasp that at the core of his addiction, it has nothing to do with sex. If you are part of his support system please be patient with him during this process because this will take time. If you are reading this chapter and you are the struggler, be patient and graceful with yourself. It took years to build these walls and it will take time to take them down. This chapter and the next will be dealing with core or foundational issues. When working on the foundation of an existing house, you have to be very careful.

The walls we will be reviewing are erected out of our wounds of the past. Each time we are wounded by others or through self-inflicted wounds, there is a message attached to that wound. Over time there may be thousands of messages. If there is no system in place to deal with these wounds or messages, they start to become themes that connect and these themes become the walls of fear we hide behind. These walls become barriers which keep us from enjoying our intimacy with God and others. The longer these barriers stay in place the more vulnerable we become to temptation.

There are two key sets of verses that will be our guides through this chapter of recovery. The first of the two is 2 Corinthians 10: 4-5. It reads, "*The weapons we fight with are not the weapons of the world. On the contrary, they have divine power to demolish strongholds. We demolish arguments and every pretension that sets itself up against the knowledge of God, and we take captive every thought to make it obedient to Christ."*

The second verse comes from Psalm 51: 6, *"Surely you desire truth in the inner parts; you teach me wisdom in the inmost place."* In the verses from 2 Corinthians we focus on these key words: strongholds, arguments, and pretension.

As a sex addict progresses in their recovery they will reach a point where they will need help in identifying their barriers to intimacy with God. They will also need help in understanding how to do spiritual warfare in order to take down these barriers. These strongholds, arguments and pretensions are things that don't agree with God's Truth and keep us from "walking in agreement with God". In the previous chapter, we discussed the addict needing to go through a process of revival. Part of an effective revival involves learning spiritual warfare. This is never clearer than in the area of sexual sin. It is important in this stage of recovery because if the addict is going to experience true healing and be empowered to confront temptation, the walls that block God's Truth must come down. We will look at some examples of these walls in just a moment but first let's look at the second passage in Psalm 51. God desires his truth to penetrate to our inner most parts. In other words, down to the core of who we are. If the walls are not taken down then the recovery process will come to a complete stop because these walls will not allow His Truth to penetrate and touch the heart of the addict.

As we walk through this section we will place these walls into 3 categories as well look at how they might act as barriers, thieves and/or compulsions. Before we begin this process, let me point out that the addict will need his support system whom should have already been formulated. Specifically, his counselor and or pastor will play a key part in helping him identify his walls. In working with sex addicts in intensive workshops I have found this area is where most addicts get stuck, arrive there too quickly, or don't seek help with this area. This section can be very frustrating for the addict because he must trust others and God, and this section may take the most time to work through. This area can also be difficult for the counselor because working with the addict once a week may make it difficult to find these walls or barriers. It is in this area that I most often recommend the addict do some intensive work. This intensive work may be done by having larger blocks of time in counseling or through intensive workshops. In once a week individual counseling for 1 hour, most of this time is spent in regaining ground the addict may have lost because of the past week's stress and temptations. There are only a few moments left to explore this area. In most cases, it is not safe to explore this area at the end of counseling because the addict may leave the session more vulnerable to temptation than when he came into the office. Residential programs or ministries can be very beneficial in providing the addict a larger block of time in a safe, structured and God-centered environment. These can allow him time to detoxify more thoroughly from his addiction and the chaos of his life as well as learn to hear God's voice again. The addict may be able to work through these issues without the use of residential care or intensive counseling. If he is able to set aside blocks of time each day in a safe environment where he will be working on counselor directed assignments then this "set aside" time approach may work as well. Whatever the approach in dealing with this area, the bottom line, once again, is this will take time and the pace and tempo must be through prayer and the direction of the Holy Spirit.

Let's return to the defining strongholds, arguments and pretensions and how they become barriers, thieves and compulsions. We will try to come up with a working definition for each one and give some examples of what they might look like in the life of an addict. We will not be able to identify all of the examples and some of the ones we review will not fit your situation. The reason for that was stated in the very early part of this book and that is: every addict's relationship with his addiction is different. This statement is especially true in this chapter and the one that will follow.

Let us first start by defining barriers, thieves, and compulsions. These definitions will not come from Webster's but we will form a working definition which will fit our purpose and pursuit of recovery. What is a *barrier*? Very simply put, a barrier is something that blocks or prohibits movement or passage. What is a *thief*? A thief is someone, or in this case something, that robs or steals something from someone that belongs to the person. What is a *compulsion*? For this discussion, we will describe a compulsion as something that drives or pushes you in a direction you do not wish to go or experience.

Let us now venture into defining and understanding what strongholds are and how they affect the recovery process of the sexually addicted. The best way I know how to describe a stronghold is through a word picture. Have you ever seen a fully mature tree growing off the side of a mountain or steep incline? Without seeing the root system of this tree, it is obvious from the external product, the tree has a very firm and established root structure. In other words, this tree has a strong hold upon this mountain. You may pass this tree for many years and it weathers various types of stressors. In some cases when the tree finally gives way to the stress, it takes part of the mountain with it as it falls.

Such is the case with the sex addict. The most obvious stronghold in the addict's life can be his sexual addiction. The tree analogy would easily fit here. The mature tree would represent the sinful behavior and the root system comes from the seeds that were planted many years before. When this stronghold of sin is exposed it sometimes has the same dramatic effect as the tree taking out the side of a mountain. There are other strongholds, however, which are not sexual but also need to be dealt with because of their potential to promote relapse. Let's take a look at one of the most prevalent strongholds an addict might have to address.

Pride can be a huge stronghold in the addict's life. A prideful root system produces a prideful tree. Even if you cut down the prideful tree the root system will produce another, and sometimes even stronger, prideful tree. This stronghold will bring the addict's recovery to a screeching halt, even if they have addressed each of the previous steps. The brokenness the addict initially experienced will cut this tree down but as time passes and the short-term memory loss kicks in, the prideful tree grows back. The addict forgets what his self-direction and pride cost him and he starts directing his own life again. The stronghold of pride will become a barrier which blocks him from fully leaning on God in everything. This barrier will prohibit or restrict the flow of God's Truth and Grace into his inner most parts. The process of sanctification will be restricted or even prohibited because of the stronghold of pride. The use of accountability partners will be blocked because the prideful person doesn't want to be told what to do. This stronghold also steals or robs from the addict the blessings that come with being used by God as his servant. Because the prideful person cannot admit to failure or pain, the addict will once again begin carrying these burdens. The longer he carries these burdens, the greater the drive or compulsion to seek relief from his pain will become.

You see the hard part about recovery is learning to walk out your healing in humility. This may be the primary reason men tend to stay sober for about 3 to 6 months following an event of brokenness and then relapse. Their pride tree grows back. If you have ever seen a "stump grinder" work on the stump of a tree you would agree this machine provides a very aggressive service in removing a stump. The stump grinder has a large circular blade which is placed upon the stump. While the blade is turning at a high rate of speed it is worked back and forth across the surface of the exposed stump. The operator will work his way into the tap root of the tree until nothing is left but a pile of sawdust. If the tree was very large this process could take quite a while. The same thing is true in removing any type of stronghold. Some of the addict's strongholds may have been there a long time and may be deeply rooted. This process should not be as intrusive and violent as the stump grinder but can be a slow and sometimes painful process.

Proverbs 27:17 [17] *As iron sharpens iron, so a man sharpens the countenance of his friend.* (NKJV)

The addict will need men in his army to provide the "iron sharpening iron" service. These men will be there to challenge him to walk in the humility of being a Godly man. A phrase I often tell those in recovery is "remember the pain but release the shame." Whatever the stronghold, the addict will need Godly men to challenge him and encourage him to bring these issues into the Light of God's Truth, not once, but continuously. His accountability questions should reflect whether he is doing this on a daily basis. Once again, the challenging of the male addict needs to come from other males. Other examples of strongholds that are often part an addict's world are: shame, guilt, self-condemnation, anger/rage, self-pity, fear, false beliefs and co-dependency.

Let's return back to our old friend Bobby. Bobby hit several "bottoms" where his stronghold of sexual addiction tree was cut down. Bobby also had strongholds of shame and pride. His core shame told him that he would never be as good as his father and he would never gain his father's approval. His stronghold of pride told him he knew all the answers and he could do it on his own. To those around him, his wall of pride told them he had it together and was in need of nothing. The combination of his shame and pride kept him from fully putting himself into accountability. They also became the fertilizer that promoted the growth and re-growth of his sexual addiction tree. His pride and shame blocked him from having true intimacy with God and others. They kept him in a place of isolation and loneliness. They robbed him of the joy and peace of his salvation. Finally, they drove him into the familiar place of his addiction.

Our next wall we will review is arguments. Arguments are not as ingrained and powerful as a stronghold but they do a significant amount of damage. Very simply put, arguments are anything that doesn't agree with God and become debates or excuses for not being obedient to Him. I call these "I ain't gonna do it!" arguments or debates with God. This often leads into complaining, griping and pity parties. Good examples of this behavior are witnessed through the Israelites in the desert. They griped, argued and complained about everything to the point of wanting to return to slavery. These arguments often come into play in the addict's recovery process when the addict needs to forgive someone who has hurt him, but the other person is not repentant. They want to argue why they "ain't gonna do it" and present a very good case for not forgiving this person. This, however, becomes an argument with God because the Bible commands us to forgive just as we have been forgiven and it is not based upon the other person's response or our feelings.

Ephesians 4:32 *And be kind to one another, tenderhearted, forgiving one another, even as God in Christ forgave you.* (NKJV)

Grief may also become a point of argument. The recovery process may be hindered when the addict is asked to grieve something painful he never grieved. They begin to feel better because they have started to get some sobriety under their belt. They believe they are past the pain they experienced from their brokenness. Then God, sometimes through the aid of their counselor, shows them areas of loss or wounds which need to be grieved. They begin to argue with God and ask "why" questions about His purpose in dragging up the past. He complains that God is cruel. Instead of grieving, he has a very fine pity party. This argument prohibits the addict's movement or recovery. It blocks the blessing God wants to give him because he won't trust God with his pain. It steals time and energy from the addict because the Holy Spirit's conviction won't let him sleep at night. Finally, his pity party leads him to a place of anger toward God because he believes God doesn't care about his pain. That anger drives him into the addiction where he can escape and instantly medicate his pain.

Let's tie these arguments into our Bobby story. Bobby carried resentments toward his father because he felt the church was more important than he was. He also picked up numerous resentments along the way because he perceived his father only cared about how he performed and not about him. These resentments culminated in him resenting his father for dying just when he was about to get his father's approval. He had never grieved his father's death because he never allowed himself to face the reality of his pain. When God, through his counselor, would approach the area of forgiveness and grieving his losses, he would debate the need for such a process because, after all, his father was a Godly man. He would excuse the need to grieve because, after all, his father was in a better place and he should be rejoicing and not sad. Privately, Bobby would create his own pity party where he blamed everyone, including God, for the "unfair" situations in his life. These pity parties kept him in a place of self-focus. Over time as he stayed in this place of arguing with God and continuous pity parties, his stronghold of pride remerged. These arguments became barriers to intimacy with God and others. They robbed him of receiving affirmation from God and the men in his support system. Finally, these arguments drove him back to the strongholds in his life.

Our next wall is the area of pretensions. Pretensions are areas of entitlement in our lives that promote an unwillingness to fully surrender everything to God. If you will remember, the first step to recovery is brokenness. The addict cannot function in life in his initial state of brokenness. From brokenness, he moves into a stage of humility and surrender. This is where God teaches about total dependency upon Him on a daily basis. The addict has to daily surrender his will over to God. The old hymn, "I Surrender All" is often a song we associate with the salvation experience. We sing it once, go down front, get saved and it really doesn't apply to us anymore. If we completely understand the concept of being a "bond servant to Christ", then we realize we must surrender everything and that includes our rights. When we become aware of the depravity of our sin nature then we lose the desire to direct and control our own lives. We surrender our rights to retaliate, self-worth, independence, pride, and self-determination. This type of surrender sounds un-

American. As Americans, we are taught from an early age we have rights. As Christians, we should understand God's plan and path for us is immensely better than anything we could dream up. If we understand God is Love and he evidenced his Love through his Son, then surrendering everything including our rights becomes less egregious. The basic question for every Christian is "who is going to drive my boat today?" Picture the addict's journey of recovery as a river voyage. The addict begins the journey in an ill-equipped raft. He is able to hold this raft together until he rounds a bend and finds himself in a horrific series of rapids. He crashes against the rocks and begins to drown. He cries for help and at the last moment is rescued. This part of his journey represents his state of brokenness when everything comes apart. He knows he must turn over the controls of his raft (his life) to God or he will die. As he passes the state of brokenness he leaves the rapids and finds smooth water. After a while he forgets the rapids. He is feeling good. Gradually, he begins to place his hand upon the controls of his raft and before long; he is the captain of his boat. The most dangerous time of recovery for the addict is when the "good times" or positive emotions return. His sense of entitlement begins to gradually move him toward directing his life. He feels entitled to do the things that all the other guys are doing. "Hey, I'm a grown man. I can watch TV anytime I want. I don't need a baby sitter while on the computer. It's embarrassing telling the guys at work I can't go to the sports bar to watch the game. They think I'm hen-pecked." These thoughts of entitlement will become arguments we have with God and others. "I don't need to be accountable for my time. Who does my wife think she is? She's not my mother or the boss of me. I ain't gonna do it. I wear the pants in this family." These arguments lead to pity parties where the addict feels sorry for himself for not having rights. This pity party will drive him into his stronghold of pride and eventually his addiction where he feels in control. In the fantasy world of his addiction, he is in control and he always feels like a man. Entitlements become barriers that block us from fully understanding the benefit of total dependency upon the Lord. They steal from us our child-like faith and security which comes in resting in his Love and direction for our lives. Finally, it drives us back to the familiar but unwanted places of our past. Let me stress something very strongly. Recovery is not the process of emasculating the male sex addict. Being a Godly masculine man means fully submitting to our Father's will and understanding and accepting the limitations of my frail human existence.

When Bobby lost his ministry career to his addiction, he took a sales job where he traveled a lot and he began to struggle with an attitude of entitlement. When he landed an account, he had worked on for several weeks, he felt entitled to reward himself. After all he had lost so much and wasn't he entitled to enjoy himself? He began to compromise small boundaries at first. He promised his wife and others he would not watch TV in his hotel room. Wouldn't it be ok to watch a basketball game? He would debate with himself it was not a big deal and it would help him with his sales because his customers were all into the March Madness thing. He always felt left out of the conversations about the games and he was sure the guys thought he was strange because he didn't watch TV. This triggered his stronghold of shame because he never felt like a man anyway. After more compromised boundaries, he eventually escaped into his addiction where he always felt like a man.

Taking Down the Walls and Opening Up the Conduit

Developing a plan of action to address taking down these walls and removing the barriers to intimacy can be difficult. There is no magic formula that will identify an addict's walls and barriers. Therefore, there is no magic or "one size fits all" approach to taking these walls down. Let's refer back to our 2 key passages of scripture. The first is 2 Corinthians 10: 4-5, *"The weapons we fight with are not the weapons of the world. On the contrary, they have divine power to demolish strongholds. We demolish arguments and every pretension that sets itself up against the knowledge of God, and we take captive every thought to make it obedient to Christ."* These 2 verses use some very strong words such as; fight, demolish, take captive and make obedient. Before we can use these strong terms we first need to understand what the weapons are that we fight with. These weapons are identified in Ephesians 6.

Ephesians 6:10-18 [10] *Finally, my brethren, be strong in the Lord and in the power of His might.* [11] *Put on the whole armor of God, that you may be able to stand against the wiles of the devil.* [12] *For we do not wrestle against flesh and blood, but against principalities, against powers, against the rulers of the darkness of this age, against spiritual hosts of wickedness in the heavenly places.* [13] *Therefore take up the whole armor of God, that you may be able to withstand in the* *evil day, and having done all, to stand. [14] Stand therefore, having girded your waist with truth, having put on the breastplate of righteousness, [15] and having shod your feet with the preparation of the gospel of peace; [16] above all, taking the shield of faith with which you will be able to quench all the fiery darts of the wicked one. [17] And take the helmet of salvation, and the sword of the Spirit, which is the word of God; [18] praying always with all prayer and supplication in the Spirit, being watchful to this end with all perseverance and supplication for all the saints* (NKJV)

A primary technique the sex addict will need to learn is how to do spiritual warfare. He will need a spiritual mentor who will instruct him and hold him accountable in developing these techniques. Before he can utilize these weapons, he must understand who he is and what his real identity is. The world has taught the addict his identity is based upon his performance, relationships and appearance. In other words, he has learned to be a "human doer" and doesn't know how to be a "human being". He has learned to build a façade of being all together. He will first need to learn what his real identity in Christ is. If he is going to fight, demolish, take captive and make obedient then those words need to be empowered. They can only be empowered by the authority of who he is in Christ. For example, if an addict has a stronghold of shame which has been there his entire life; he can only demolish this deeply rooted tree with the "stump grinder" of God's truth. It is amazing to me how many long-standing Christians there are who don't have a clue who they really are. The non-sex addict Christian may function fairly well without ever having the full understanding of who they really are. For the Christian sex addict, it is imperative they not only know who they are in Christ but also how this knowledge empowers the work of spiritual warfare.

The sex addict has to put on "the belt of Truth" every day by committing to complete honesty. He needs to know how to guard his thoughts with the "knowledge of his salvation" because without it, his thoughts will lead him to the places of shame and regret. His heart needs to be guarded with the "Breastplate of Righteousness" so he knows he is right with God and his "inner most parts" are protected. He needs to learn how to use the "Shield of Faith" to extinguish the fiery darts of Satan's lies of fear, hopelessness and despair. He needs to set aside his faulty shield of faith which was based upon faith in him or others. He needs to understand how to use the "Sword of Truth" as both an offensive and defensive weapon. He needs to understand what it means to be "shod with the Gospel of Peace" and not stirring up chaos and strife wherever he goes.

When it comes to warfare there are 2 components which are very helpful for the warrior to develop. The warrior needs a warrior's attitude and the ability to use pre-emptive and pro-active strikes. A warrior's attitude say's, "I am sick and tired of Satan robbing and stealing from me and I'm drawing a line in the sand." This attitude comes from the place of understanding God's grace is sufficient to cover his sins and he is walking in full agreement with God's Truth that he is forgiven. This understanding is not based upon "cheap" grace but from the full understanding of the depravity of his sin and also the full covering of His mercy and grace. The addict begins to "separate the sin from the sinner" by walking in agreement with the truth. The truth states his real identity is not based upon what he has done, good or bad, but upon what was done for him through the redemptive blood of Christ. This truth provides his warrior's attitude with empowerment. This new attitude is turned toward the author of his sin and all lies and that is Satan. When Satan comes at the addict with the shame and condemnation of the past sins, he can point to Romans 8:1 and take captive those thoughts with authority and power. The more the addict practices spiritual warfare the more open his conduit between him and God becomes. Through this process, he begins to develop a pre-emptive and proactive approach to warfare. In other words, he can, as my grandmother would say, "see trouble coming from a mile away." This approach makes him vigilant and when any strongholds, arguments or pretensions come at him, he is ready to demolish and take captive any of them with God's Truth.

Let me give you a visual image of what we are discussing. The recovering sex addict is driving down the road of life and he is "walking in agreement with who he is in Christ". He is enjoying the peace and contentment which comes with his intimacy with God. He comes to a "T" in the road with the fearful message of shame and failure looming before him. If he turns right he will still be in agreement with God's Truth that he is forgiven. If he turns left, he will be allowing this message of fear into his "inner most part". He will disconnect from his intimacy with God because this message does not agree with God. This message can come from someone very close or someone distant. This message can come from a place of reality or perception. The more the recovering addict chooses to turn right and stay in agreement with God, the better his warrior's attitude becomes. This warfare becomes most difficult in situations I call "big dog situations". Big dog situations are ones where there is a lot riding on the situation or the other person in the situation is very close to the addict. Examples of this occur frequently with married recovering addicts. This can occur in a situation as small as the garbage not being taken out and the spouse is trying to express her disappointment. The situation is small but it is a big dog situation to the addict because his wife's opinion carries a lot of weight. The addict may see the message coming at him before she even says anything because he recognizes the tension in her shoulders and the deep sigh she displays as he enters the room. If he is prepared, he will see this situation as an opportunity to assault the old lie that he is a failure. If he turns to the right on the road of life, then there can be freedom in the conversation with his wife. He can acknowledge he failed in his performance but he is not a failure. If he turns to the left, then his conduit to God will begin to be blocked because he is now listening to a lie that doesn't agree with God and he is placing his wife's approval above God's.

Galatians 1:10 *For do I now persuade men, or God? Or do I seek to please men? For if I still pleased men, I would not be a bondservant of Christ.* (NKJV)

He will become defensive and there will be no freedom in the conversation. Often, the spouse interprets this defensiveness as him being secretive and he must be covering up more than just the lack of garbage maintenance. She becomes afraid and begins interrogating the addict. His walls become higher because he feels judged and misunderstood. This scene can go back and forth for a long period of time until both the spouse and the addict are fully entrenched behind their defensive walls. This garbage can incident my sound a bit silly but this is from a real situation which led to the addict's relapse. The well-trained spiritual-warrior- recovering-sex addict views these situations as opportunities to take old lies and make them obedient to God's Truth. He recognizes that this is not about having everyone's approval. The well-trained warrior can be preemptive and proactive and can act in a situation of stress and not react.

Let's go back to Bobby's story and the incident which occurred during his little league baseball game. If we follow the track where Bobby lost the game, then it was a big dog situation which carried a powerful message that he was a failure and everyone rejected him because of this failure. Because he did not receive the tool in his tool box of how to deal with this pain, he internalized his pain and began to build walls of protection. The message of this event connected with other events with the same message. This connection became a theme or false belief he filtered future events through. These themes or lies became barriers to intimacy with God, himself and others. When Bobby moved into adulthood and became a full-blown sex addict, he would hit several periods of brokenness followed by a period of sobriety. During these times of sobriety, he would continue to receive messages which sounded like failure and rejection from his wife and others. He still did not have the tools to deal with these messages. He did know, however, how to survive by building walls of protection to keep from getting hurt. These walls gave the appearance he was doing okay but behind the walls he carried the burdens of loneliness and pain.

So, how do you deal with these messages? In developing a support team for dealing with this area, there are 2 people which can be very beneficial. The first has already been alluded to and that is a pastor who is gifted in instructing practical techniques for spiritual warfare. The second is a Christian therapist/counselor who is trained in the area of cognitive therapy. These 2 people need to be in communication and on the same page with one another. This can become tricky because the addict may begin his counseling with a counselor who treats sexual addiction but is not trained in or comfortable with cognitive therapy. Often times the addiction counselor will refer to a cognitive therapist for some intensive work while still remaining in the recovering addict's program. There is no specific time line for when the recovering addict is ready to deal with his barriers. Some are ready within a few months and others it may take a few years. This does not mean that the recovering addict is stagnant in his recovery or miserable. It means God is preparing him for this procedure. Taking down these walls can be very painful and he needs to know he can trust God even when he allows hurt into his life. God spoke to Elijah in a whisper or still small voice because he didn't want to frighten him. Even though the process of taking down these walls can be painful, it is also very delicate work because we are talking about issues of the heart. Some of the walls are built around traumas such sexual abuse, emotional incest, physical and spiritual abuse. Jesus came to set the captives free and to bind the broken hearted. The walls were built out of self-protection and survival mode but over time they trap the addict behind a wall of despair. The walls are not taken down with a bulldozer but with the loving hands of The Carpenter who takes them down one brick at a time. With each brick removed, he whispers to the wounded soul of the addict, "I love you, yes, even you."

Chapter 6

Dealing with the Core Issues

I have heard on several occasions Dr. James Dobson refer to a story about a Walleye fish that is placed into a large aquarium. The fish has free reign of the entire tank and when minnows are placed in the tank he quickly consumes them. A clear Plexiglas wall is placed around the fish and then the minnows are added to the tank on the outside of this wall. The fish violently attacks the minnows but is met with the painful and abrupt impact of the wall he is unable to see. The fish eventually stops striking at the minnows because the pain of having his needs not met is greater than the risk he would take to meet his need for nourishment. The wall surrounding the fish is removed and now the minnows swim right in front of the fish's mouth but he does not move or attempt to have his need met. The fish has reached a place of despair and hopelessness. His need to consume minnows is a core need of this fish but he has given up and believes his need will never be met again. Even though, in reality, there is a feast of minnows around him which would more than meet his need, the fish starves to death. A fish is fairly simple and basic regarding his needs. He does not require other fish to affirm or validate him. He doesn't get his feelings hurt if another fish doesn't choose him for fish games. Humans, on the other hand, are most likely the neediest of all of God's creation. We have emotional, spiritual, psychological, mental, physical, and relational needs. We place high importance and expectations upon these needs to such a level where disappointment is almost always certain. Sometimes this disappointment occurs when others cut off or block this need from being met and other times they don't have the ability to meet our needs. We have already discussed earlier in the book how we might become wounded and so we will not retrace these steps. In this chapter, our goal is to address the "heart of the issue" or to get at the core issues or needs that drive the sexual addiction. In the last chapter, we discussed the need to take down the walls or barriers to intimacy with God and others. Taking down these walls allows God's Truth to penetrate to our inner most parts or our hearts. Even though we are much more complicated than a fish, we often respond as the fish in the story. After experiencing repeated pain in having our needs unmet we will often stop trying even though there is a feast swimming around us. Once the walls begin to be taken down, the recovering addict will need to place himself in relationships with other men who will be conduits of God's love and truth for him. The accountability men who were referred to earlier can be of an assist here or there may be other men of grace God places in his life. As I write this chapter I am presently spiritually mentoring a young man. He has in place an active accountability system consisting of a therapist, 2 support groups, accountability questions, a primary group of supportive men, and has attended an intensive workshop. He has a working understanding of sobriety and his barriers to intimacy. He is at a point where he recognizes his earthly father cannot meet certain needs and he needs to be proactive in having these needs filled. He was proactive in asking me to address his spiritual need to be mentored or "fathered". He has asked other men to address his unmet emotional needs. I often view God as an economist. He is always balancing things. I have observed when someone is wounded relationally then God uses relationships to balance out the needs of the individual. Several years ago, I was providing a workshop for a man who struggled with unwanted same sex internet pornography. He was a professional, married, respected in his community and very involved in his church. At the beginning of a workshop, I always have the men tell their life story. Sometimes this rehashing of their lives takes several hours and sometimes an entire day. He was a few hours into his story and was well into his adolescent years when I stopped him. He had not mentioned his father one time in the first 18 years of his life. I asked him if his father was dead or if his parents had divorced. He stated his father was indeed alive and his parents were still married. His father had no impact in his life, either harmful or beneficial. His father was a non-entity in his life. In other words, he had never been fathered. As his workshop progressed, we begin to pray for God to place into his life someone who could and would "father him." Little did we know, back at his home church, an older man was meeting with his pastor and telling him God was moving him to "father" someone. For the next 4 years God used this older man as a conduit of His love to "restore the years the locusts had taken." This father figure did not understand nor was he trained in the area of sexual addiction but he knew how to father. This fathering process promoted the recovering addict's ability to forgive his natural father for the non-intrusive wounds he had left with his son. Once again, God is an economist. When he began to release his resentments and unmet needs of the past, God was there to fill the void and not leave him with an empty hand. This story almost sounds too simple and magical regarding its outcome. We prayed and "poof", God met the need. Let me assure you this is not the case. There were years of secrecy with repeated relapses and pledges to never return to his sin. This recovering addict had followed a path of recovery that had taken several years. God led him through a process which took down his barriers of fear and pride that kept him trapped and desperate for his father's love. In God's perfect timing, he provided His "love in skin" through this humble and obedient older believer.

I have never witnessed God drop the ball when it comes to meeting the core needs of recovering addicts. I have, however, observed recovering addicts who could not or would not receive these gifts. They become the Walleye fish who starved to death even though there were provisions for their needs all around them. In many cases the addict may not know what they are missing regarding their core needs. They had never experienced having these needs met and so therefore they had no reference point. Most often the addict will need someone to validate the need they are pursuing is normal, healthy and valid. They will need encouragement to take the risk in having their needs met. Healthy people ask for what they need within clearly defined expectations from safe people. Giving guidance to the addict will help him formulate what his core needs are with healthy expectations. Without this guidance, the addict may place all of his needs into one relational "basket". If you are going to go fishing you have to go to a pond, because they won't be delivered to your house. The recovering addict will need to go where the "fish" are located.

Finding these relational fish may involve joining a men's Sunday school class, or a men's prayer breakfast. When assisting the recovering person as a counselor or pastor, one of the best ways to help is to listen to his life story. As you listen to his story, record the unmet needs he had throughout his life. This will assist you in developing a plan of how and where he can meet these needs. If the time is not taken to listen then often times the "shotgun method" is used. This occurs when we throw people into as many church activities as possible and hope their needs get met. This can frustrate the addict because they become overwhelmed with the time that is consumed by this approach and it is not very personal. I was counseling with a middle-aged pastor several years ago who had been walking in sobriety for quite a while and was working through some of the wounds of his past. He identified one of his wounds was his father had never taken him fishing but would always take his brother. As he grieved this loss and forgave his father he realized God had been providing him a very specific way to fill this need. He had a member of his church ask him repeatedly to take this pastor and his son fishing. This was a very gracious and kind man who would not ridicule him for his lack of fishing abilities. The only thing that kept him from receiving this invite was his fear of failure and rejection. Once these barriers or walls were taken down he could now take the risk to receive this gift. When we finished our time together, I challenged him to take the risk of letting this man take him fishing. When we talked on the phone about one month later he sounded like a kid who just learned how to ride a bike. He reported, with joy and excitement he had indeed gone fishing with this man and he was most likely the worst fisherman in the world but he didn't care. He realized going fishing with his friend had nothing to do with fish. He realized God was using this Godly man to fill some very important core needs. At the core of his being, he needed to know that he was special, unique and chosen. He knew from his theological training, God loved him in this manner and Christ chose to die for him. He knew he was special in God's eyes and God had truly made him with unique gifts. God also knew he needed this confirmed through the love and fellowship of another believer. In other words, he needed "Jesus in skin." Once again, this event of receiving this gift did not occur over night. This man had to first receive in his core God loved him in this special way. This unconditional love from God, received at the core of his existence, set the foundation for him to enjoy God's gift which he provided through the simple act of fishing. If he had sought out meeting this need only through his friend's gesture then he would have been seeking the approval of man. The fishing trip would have been a failure because he would have been basing this approval upon his ability to perform and after all he did fail as a fisherman.

God is always more concerned about changing the hearts of men. He also desires to be the father to the fatherless, to bind the broken hearted and for us to experience the childlike joy of intimacy with Him. When God gets to the place of dealing with the addict's core needs or his heart, he is dealing with the tap root of the kudzu plant of the addiction. The stump grinder has already demolished the stronghold of the tree of sexual addiction and now He is filling the empty hole left behind with His love. Every Christian wants to experience God's love this deeply but we don't want the pain. If you are reading this book and are the struggling sex addict, I present this chapter as a message of hope. God does heal, restore and make anew. If you are struggling and looking for the quick, easy and painless rout then you need to back up because there is a journey you have yet to take. If you are the loved one or a support person of the addict and believe that merely surrounding the addict with good people will change them then he may follow the path of the Walleye. You may be the spouse of the addict and God has shown years ago your husband's core issues are but he just won't listen. He has to go on his own journey of recovery in order to receive what God has already revealed to you. I mentioned at the beginning of this book, every addict's relationship with their sexual sin is different. This is especially true when it comes to the core needs. One addict's core needs may center on the needs of being special, unique and chosen. Others may have the core need for approval or validation. As the addict progresses through the journey of healing and recovery, God will reveal these needs according to His perfect timing and intimate knowledge of his child. Once again this is process or a journey and not an event. The journey can be hard and painful at times but the blessing and the filling of His living water is more than worth it. Only God's living water can touch the dead places of our heart and bring them to life. When God fills our voids with his love and compliments it with the gift of Godly fellowship, then the desire to pursue the counterfeit offerings of the world is diminished.

Chapter 7

The Blessing of the Thorn

2 Corinthians 12:8-10 [8] *Concerning this thing I pleaded with the Lord three times that it might depart from me.* [9] *And He said to me, "My grace is sufficient for you, for My strength is made perfect in weakness." Therefore, most gladly I will rather boast in my infirmities, that the power of Christ may rest upon me.* [10] *Therefore I take pleasure in infirmities, in reproaches, in needs, in persecutions, in distresses, for Christ's sake. For when I am weak, then I am strong.* (NKJV)

Toward the end of chapter one, I introduced the concept of sexual addiction being a thorn in the flesh. After that introduction, I left you hanging and did not present the blessings which comes with embracing the thorn of sexual addiction. The delay in presenting these blessings is due to the preparation process God takes the addict through in order for them to fully receive these blessings. Remember back when we discussed the planting of the seeds of sexual addiction? The soil that received the seeds of sexual addiction required preparation and timing. The same is true for the recovery process. The recovering addict's heart, which is the soil, has to be prepared and God's timing followed. The stony heart of the addict has to be broken and prepped for the seeds of God's blessing.

Let us now return to the issue of the thorn in the flesh. Paul pleaded with the Lord repeatedly to remove this thorn of torment from his life. Finally, after some undisclosed period of time Jesus spoke to him. There appears to be an implied "No" in Jesus response.

He will not be removing this thorn. We do not know if Jesus removed it later but Paul does not mention it in any other writings. This thorn also did not define who Paul was or who he was going to be. The thorn was a vehicle God used to bless Paul and to glorify Himself. The same holds true for the sexual addiction thorn in the flesh. If the addict will embrace his thorn in the flesh, his complete powerlessness to remove it and Jesus' implied "No" to remove it, then he can follow a journey where he will be blessed. If the addict can grasp that God is using the addiction as a vehicle to bless him then he may realize his addiction has nothing to do with inappropriate sexual behavior. I have seen many struggling addicts develop a significant resentment toward God because of his implied "No" regarding removing their sexual addiction. Their resent toward God hardens their hearts and the seeds of the blessings are not received. This resentful addict may be able to maintain long periods of sobriety and in some cases never return to his addiction. He will, however, miss something very special that comes with the blessings of the thorn.

Let us now address the first blessing. In verse 9, Jesus finally spoke to Paul and first said "My grace is sufficient," The first blessing Christ wants to give is the understanding that his grace is sufficient to cover the entirety of the sexual addict's sins. As well as providing the grace to deal with his daily struggles. As the sex addict inventories the costs of his sins, he needs to know he has not exceeded God's grace, mercy and forgiveness. This concept sounds wonderful and fairly basic regarding theology. I have found most Christians, however, have a very limited or superficial understanding of grace or an inaccurate one. This is especially true with the Christian sexual addict. I have seen many ministers that provided an accurate presentation of God's grace to others but because of their sexual sin could not receive what they gave to others. One of the mistakes we often make in addressing the concept of grace is to uncouple grace from truth. Let's refer back to scripture in John chapter 1. Verse 14 says, *"The Word became flesh and made his dwelling among us. We have seen his glory, the glory of the One and Only, who came from the Father, full of grace and truth."* Now let's skip down to verses 16 and 17, *"From the fullness of his grace we have all received one blessing after another. For the law was given through Moses; grace and truth came through Jesus Christ."* You see God did not send his Son to uncouple truth from grace but instead he sent him to bring union to them. The truth is we can never meet God's expectations that were presented to Moses. When Jesus came, and dwelt among us he even raised the standard of God's expectations by looking straight into the hearts of men and exposing the depravity David described in Psalm 51. When I was in high school the Soviet Union still existed. In the area of track and field there was a great race to see who could clear the height of 20 feet in pole vaulting. The United States had their star and the Soviet's had theirs. I believe the Soviet star cleared the height first and others have since followed in his footsteps. The Law of Moses is similar to the bar being set at 20 feet. The people came to believe if they followed the rules close enough then they could clear the bar and make it into heaven. In other words, they viewed the Law through the eyes of "I can work my way into Heaven". The religious leaders had raised the bar of expectations, not through God's direction, but to make themselves powerful and rich. Jesus stepped into the world speaking with the full authority of his father and raised the bar. From that point, we could never live under the delusion we could clear God's bar of standards. When Jesus looks into the hearts of men, the bar no longer stays at 20 feet, it is moved beyond our sight because our attempts to meet them are at best "filthy rags." Jesus had and has the perfect balance of grace and truth. Jesus raised the bar of expectation by letting us know we can't meet the standard of perfection but he could and did. The truth that we can't meet God's standards crushes us but the coupling of God's grace, through the gift of his Son, saves us.

We live in a world today where many Christians and churches have uncoupled grace and truth. When truth is uncoupled from grace then it becomes legalism. Many recovering sex addicts struggle with a legalist relationship with themselves and sometimes with others. Many were raised in legalist churches where God's truth was used as a weapon of fear to control and manipulate the congregation. They may have been raised in a legalist home where it was more important how you appeared and performed than for what was going on inside of you. I was not raised in either one of these environments but struggled with being very legalistic with myself because of the consistent messages of shame I put upon myself. You may have witnessed on TV shows or cartoons where there was an angel on one shoulder and a devil on the other of a struggling character. What I see most of the time with recovering sex addicts is

Christ on one shoulder and a well-dressed, very articulate legalist on the other. You see the legalist is about death and he wants to kill the recovering addict's joy and peace. Have you ever tried to argue or debate a legalist? It is a waste of time and an act of futility because technically speaking the legalist is correct. Often times the addict will try to debate with the legalist on his shoulder but he always loses because the legalist is correct in assessing his degree of failure. Some addicts will try performance based techniques to silence the accusing legalist but to no avail because he can never balance the books. You see the legalist is me. I have more evidence to convict me and find me guilty than anyone else ever will. This hardened legalist part of my mind and heart needs to die and be brought into agreement with God's truth about how he sees me. The legalist will not die through performance or debating but none the less he must die. How you kill the legalist that lives within the addict is by coupling it with God's grace, mercy and forgiveness. Many addicts live within a belief system that they have exceeded God's grace because of the repetitive pattern of their addiction and all the evidence they have against themselves. The legalist within them has held court and found them guilty. Before we get to the process of killing the legalist, let's look at the other side of the coin when we uncouple truth and grace.

Grace uncoupled from truth is a license to sin. We live in the time of the "ear ticklers". The "ear tickers" always present a message that makes you feel good and brings a smile to your face. Some of the fastest growing churches in the United States are what I call the "happy-slappy-sappy" churches. They are the churches that never talk about sin and its cost because it might make someone feel bad. Just like the legalist, technically what they are teaching is true. They teach that God is love and that he wants the best for you and that no one should perish. This is true. Grace uncoupled from truth is cheap grace and minimizes the price paid for this gift. This cheap grace theology promotes the belief that God wants me to be happy and I have a right to pursue what makes me happy because it is his will and desire for me. I have seen many addicts approach recovery with this cheap grace mind set. When you ask them to be completely honest about the ugliness of their sin, they hide behind statements such as, "Well, that's under the blood and we don't need to talk about that. As far as the east is from the west, my sins are departed from me. We leave the past behind us and press on toward the goal that God has set before us." All these statements are scripturally based but often times they are telling these things to their wives within hours of being discovered in their sexual sin. The addict will not only miss the blessing which comes with this misuse of grace but he can also use it as a defense and sometimes a weapon. The addict will need to learn to grieve the costs of his sin because that is part of the repentance and restoration process. Cheap grace will not allow this process to occur because embracing pain indicates a lack of faith in one's inability to receive the wealth and prosperity plan for your life. Just as with the legalist, this message of cheap grace must die. The mortification of this theology occurs through the coupling of truth to grace. When truth is applied, then sin becomes sin and not a mistake. Cheap grace minimizes sin in a similar way that legalism maximizes sin. We seek the balance of grace and truth of which Christ demonstrated and carried out to perfection.

Killing the Legalist-The First Blessing

Several years ago, I worked in a Christ-centered inpatient treatment program. Through the years, we had several patients who struggled with the fear they had committed the "unpardonable sin". Initially, I was uncertain in how to respond to their struggle. I begin to read various writings on the subject of the "unpardonable sin". There were about as many opinions on what it was as there were writings. The one common link in these opinions was if you were worried you had done this sin then you had not. The reasoning behind this opinion comes with the understanding the Holy Spirit convicts believers when they are in sin or rebellion. This conviction can become very unpleasant if the believer doesn't respond. If the unpardonable sin is committed then the sinner will no longer "feel bad" about his sinning. My purpose in bringing this up is not to open the debate about whether salvation is permanent or temporal, so please try not to go there. The reason for presenting this issue is many recovering sex addicts believe they have committed the unpardonable sin and they cannot be forgiven. The legalist, which dwells within the addict, points out that not only have they sinned but they did it repeatedly and they knew better. Remember, technically speaking the legalist is correct. If you recall, the first step in recovery is honesty. This step doesn't stop after the first week of recovery. It never stops. Many addicts will do a gradual process of disclosure and honesty that may take months. This often frustrates the wife and the people supportive of his recovery. The wife will often state, "Why couldn't he just have told me everything in the beginning. Now I wait around wondering what else is he going to tell me?" There are many reasons the recovering addict may choice the path of gradual disclosure. One reason occurs when the addict "stashes" away certain events he believes are unforgivable. He has not yet allowed God into those places because of this fear and the lies which surround them. There was a young man in a support group I had facilitated for several years. He would come to the group for a period of time after being caught in pornography use and then stop until he was caught several months later and had repeated this pattern several times. His focus was to be honest with his wife about what had been discovered and focus on her forgiveness. Recently, this pattern ceased working because his sexual addiction had progressed beyond his ability to cover it up and God exposed his sin. His wife was not as quick to take him back and he was forced to bring all his sins to God and with complete honesty seek God's forgiveness and grace. The process of being totally honest and truthful with himself, others and God was very painful but he was blessed by the fact that God's grace was sufficient. His wife, parents, siblings and children's grace and forgiveness was not sufficient but His was. He is now being blessed with not only the knowledge but also the penetrating truth about God's grace which came through the gift of his Son. He now is being used as a conduit of God's grace for the other struggling men. So, how do you kill the legalist who dwells within the sexual addict? You agree with him. The legalist in the addict's brain may sound like this, "You know that 70 times 7 Jesus talked about, well you passed it a long time ago. You knew better. You were raised in a Christian home. How can you call yourself a Christian? Not only did you do this sin repeatedly, you enjoyed it, sought it and planned how to get to it more often. You abandoned your wife and family for a quick thrill. What a loser." Imagine the torment that goes on with the addict through this constant assault. The addict's response to these assaults is to agree with them. You see the legalist is the great liar himself, Satan. He takes the truth and distorts it. "You know you are right Satan. I did know better and everything you say is true but let me introduce you to my advocate or my lawyer. I believe you know him quite well and his name is Jesus. You see I gave him all of the sins you are pointing out and they now belong to him because he paid for them. So, go see my lawyer." Jesus can't fight for us until we give him our "case".

Remember, the thorn in the flesh of sexual addiction will exacerbate, accelerate, and magnify the addict's sinful nature. As it grows in the compartmentalized secret world, the sinful behavior multiplies. After years of sinful behavior, he believes he has exceeded God's grace and forgiveness. The behavior of his sin is speaking so loudly he doesn't know who he is any longer. As he is faced with the brokenness of his sinful behavior, he needs to receive the first blessing of the thorn, His Grace is sufficient to cover them all. This is not a cheap grace offered as a quick feel good response but one which is coupled with the blunt truth he failed to meet God's expectations. During his recovery process the addict will need his men of grace to tell him the truth, not minimize or maximize his sin and then point him toward God's Grace. You cannot experience the sweetness of God's Grace until you have tasted the bitterness of your sin. When we bring our sin before the Holy, Pure and Righteous God of the universe, it not only crushes us, it takes the pretty off of our sin. If a Christian sex addict can begin to walk in agreement with God's forgiveness then he can give freedom to those he has hurt to forgive when they are ready. We, as sinners, can always have vertical restoration with God. Horizontal restoration with others takes time and in some cases, will not occur.

The Christian sex addict who can receive this first blessing of grace can over time become a conduit of God's grace for others. With his understanding of how vile his heart can be but how great God's grace is, he can share that message of hope with others who have come to believe they too are unforgivable and beyond hope. We are instructed to love the unlovable. That begins with us because on our own merits we are unlovable and unworthy. It is through Christ's love and worthiness we are made whole and redeemed. This process of recovery is about revival and it begins with the individual and spreads to others. The greatest experience in the world is to be used by God. The sex addict needs to know the pain of recovery is worth the joy of God one day using them to spread the wonderful testimony of His Grace.

Weakness Equals Strength- The Second Blessing

2 Corinthians 12:9 *But he said to me "My grace is sufficient for you, and my power is made perfect in weakness."*

We live in a world where power and strength are deemed as positive attributes and something to strive for. You would be hard pressed to find someplace in this world where weakness is viewed in a positive light. Because we live in a fallen world, it is easy for Christians to adopt such a view as well. When the sexual addict hits his bottom or experiences brokenness, he realizes he is powerless and lacks the ability to fix himself. This brokenness experience, as mentioned earlier, is fundamental to his healing. The second part of the blessing of the thorn in the flesh is presented in the second half of our key verse. *"my power is made perfect in weakness."* At first glance this may appear to the addict as the experience of brokenness and his strength will return once the initial brokenness has subsided. Not only will the addict miss the second blessing but he is also going down a road which leads to relapse. This approach is much like a child who does a risky behavior and breaks his arm. The child is powerless to make his arm well and lacks the strength in that arm to perform normal activities. The child's arm heals over time and is no longer powerless and regains his strength. He may return to his risky behavior because he now knows what he did was wrong and can avoid a broken bone. This can also be the case with the recovering sex addict. Once the pain of his brokenness subsides, he returns to his risky behavior and no longer views God as someone he has to depend upon on a consistent basis.

Another factor in our world system is to teach our children to become more and more independent. The goal appears to be to raise a child who in adulthood is self-made and answers to no one.

The world tells us only the losers and failures of the world can't overcome adversity through self-will. Once again, the church often adopts this into its mindset. The prosperity movement has become very popular in today's churches. We even offer formula prayers, and a special sanctified prayer cloth that will produce success in your life and it only costs $19.95. But wait there is more! If you commit to a 15% tithing for the next year and God will return your investment 10-fold. This "stab it and grab it" approach to Christianity, says to you God doesn't want you to struggle and be unhappy. He wants to empower you and bless you with prosperity. The reality is we were adopted into God's family through the works of Jesus Christ. He wants us to learn to be his obedient and dependent children. God is not a great slot machine in the sky that if we hit the right numbers then he will pay off. In other words, God has an inverted developmental system. He wants us to become more dependent upon him and less upon ourselves. Sometimes he allows a thorn in the flesh to promote such a dependency. There are several reasons why a recovering addict might miss the second blessing. One reason is he may view God through the lens of the performance based prosperity movement. That is to say, if he does things just right then God will prosper him again. These recovering addicts will often become the "perfect" client in counseling and groups.

If Paul were alive today we might say things like, "Boy that Paul is a shaker and a mover. He knows how to get the job done. He doesn't mess around. Did you see that argument he had with Peter? You know how hard-headed Peter is and Paul put him in his place. Smart? What are talking about? That Paul is one smart cookie. He's the kind of guy you want on your team because he is going places." Paul had a lot of strengths but that is not what he boasted in. He boasted in his weakness. God allowed Satan to place a thorn in his flesh to teach him about weakness and dependency that produces strength. Once again, we have already covered the powerlessness which comes with the brokenness during the early part of recovery. The weakness Christ revealed to Paul through this thorn is the same weakness and dependency a young child experiences with their parents. Often times at this point in the recovery process the addict will begin to shut down. If the addict has not dealt with his wounds of the past and his barriers to intimacy with God, he will not be able to receive the second blessing. You see the wounds and the barriers tell him to not trust because he will be hurt. There is a check in his spirit that says, "Whoa! Stop! Time-Out! The last time I was this weak I got hurt so it is not ok to be that weak." The walls or barriers need to be taken down for this blessing to be fully received. Jesus did not say to Paul His strength was perfected in Paul's intellect, articulating abilities, scriptural knowledge or his drive. Christ's strength came to him through Paul's inability and taught him to have child-like dependency upon him. What occurred in verse 9 was an event. Christ spoke to him only once about this issue. What is written in verse 10 was more of an ongoing process in Paul's life. Paul was able to find delight in weaknesses, insults, hardships, persecutions, and difficulties. Paul found delight in being able to hold his Heavenly Father's hand because the thorn had taught him to have child-like dependency upon Him. Paul was not only insulted by those on the opposing side but he was often insulted and challenged by other believers. These insults brought him delight because they kept him in constant communication with his Daddy. Paul's hardships are well documented in scripture. He could have easily had a real nice pity party after his ship wrecked, a snake bites him and his traveling companions insult him. Instead, he delighted in these hardships because he knew his Father had a plan and he could fully trust in His plan. Paul's persecutions were many. While being chained to a Roman guard he repeatedly instructed the Philippians to rejoice and find delight in the Lord. Paul had not read the New Testament and did not know he would not die the next morning in Rome. Paul had too many difficulties to even mention. All of these situations taught him when he was weak, then he was strong.

Receiving the second blessing of weakness is a process. Just as Paul went through his life of hardships and difficulties taught him to lean fully upon the strength of the Lord. Sometimes staying in this place of dependency upon the Lord is hampered not by the difficulties of life but during the "good times". Often times the recovering sex addict will forget the need for dependency when the pain of his sexual sin becomes a distant memory. This is where ongoing accountability and the need for the addict to give back to those beginning their recovery journey is important. I have a friend who was an air traffic controller in the Navy many years ago. He said that there was a point in a plane's decent for landing the controller would direct the pilot regarding his glide path. If the plane ventured too far off this path he would direct him to vector or adjust his course a certain degree to avert danger. This illustration helps demonstrate the need for ongoing accountability to keep the recovering addict on "glide path" or with in God's will. It is within all of our human natures to want to drive our own boat. It goes back to the original sin where Satan tempted man with the desire to be independent of God's "glide path". The accountability of the men of grace challenges the recovering addict with "who is driving your boat today?" Being weak and dependent upon God on a daily basis is also linked to the process of walking in humility. Walking in dependency upon God that is linked with humility teaches us to embrace the blessings Jesus described in the beatitudes. The recovering sex addict will experience hardships and difficulties during his recovery and he will have to choose to lean upon self-reliance or God dependency. God never takes away our choice because if he does then it is not really love he receives from us. Jesus said if we loved him we would keep his commandments. It is easy for the sex addict to choose self-reliance because it fits his nature. Each time the addict choices to lean upon God during difficulties he shows his love for the Father. The most common source of difficulty the married recovering sex addict will experience will come in his interactions with his wife. Because the addict has betrayed his wife, he has little trust equity built up with his wife. When the wife questions him in areas of honesty, he becomes stressed with the difficulty that comes with this confrontation. If he tries to lean upon his own abilities to solve the conflict then he will often utilize his strengths of intellect, articulation and his scriptural knowledge. He will have missed an opportunity to lean upon God and his wife will perceive this attempt on his part as manipulation. On the other hand, if he leans upon God's strength during this difficulty then not only will he be strengthened but he can also become a conduit of God's love for his wife. You see his human love will not and cannot touch his wife's wounds. Each time the addict leans upon his Father during difficulties then he becomes a conduit of God's love to those around him. It is through this process the revival or renewal spreads to others. When the recovering addict learns to fully embrace the second blessing of the thorn in the flesh, then he will begin to understand what freedom truly looks like. He experiences freedom in his walk with the Lord because he can trust in his Father's guidance and direction for his life. He can therefore extend freedom to those around him. This concept may appear a tad bit abstract and confusing if you are just beginning the healing process. Let me give a practical example of how this might occur during an addict's recovery process. Bob is a Christian who is recovering from sexual addiction to internet pornography. He has a support system involving a support group, accountability partners and an individual counselor. He has about 3 months of sobriety from any porn use. Things appear to be going well with his wife and they have not had any major conflicts during this time of sobriety. Part of Bob's recovery plan is he will not have more than 15 minutes of unaccountable time. He is going through some hardships at work but is leaning upon God's strength to deal with the issues that arise there. He is experiencing freedom, as well as peace, regarding the stress at work. This in turn becomes a witness to his coworkers because they see the peace and freedom he is experiencing. They approach him and are curious about this "new Bob" they are seeing. This allows Bob to become a conduit of his Father's love to those he works with. One day, after work, Bob is sharing his story with a co-worker and is presenting the Gospel to him. He loses track of time and realizes he has spent 45 minutes of unaccountable time with him. In other words, he is 45 minutes late in arriving home. As he leaves work, he realizes in his hurry he left his cell phone sitting at his desk. He is unable to call his wife so his unaccountable time extends another 30 minutes because of his drive home. Remember Bob has not relapsed and was being used by God to minister to a co-worker who did not know Christ. During Bob's drive home, he will have to choose whom or what he will lean upon. If he choices to lean upon his own abilities then when he arrives home he may have a very well prepared intellectual verbal presentation which is reinforced with scripture and his duty to carry out the great commission. This presentation may be very accurate and be successful in preventing a major confrontation with his wife but he may also have missed an opportunity to be a conduit of God's love to his wife's fears and wounds. If he choices this route and his wife doesn't respond or accept his presentation then the difficulty may progress very quickly into a hardship or even a persecution by his wife. In other words, she may challenge not only his presentation and his reasoning for being late but she may question the realness of his Christian walk. What if Bob, during his drive home, choices the other option? He utilizes the second blessing of the thorn in the flesh and in his weakness, leans upon his Father. His first action might be to pray and seek his Father's guidance. He might also call one of his support people to pray with him. (That is if he had remembered his phone) He might reflect upon specific scripture verses which reassure him God is with him and is still in charge. If he leans upon the Holy Spirit's guidance then once he arrives home he might be able to give his wife the freedom to express her feelings. He might listen first to her pain and realize God can still use him as a conduit for his wife. I understand some men may read this and think this response sounds kind of "wimpy" if he would let his wife run over him. This approach is actually just the opposite. If Bob leans fully upon his identity in Christ during this difficulty then he doesn't have to have his wife's affirmation because he knows he has it with Christ. In other words, he doesn't have to become defensive with his wife. If his identity, however, is based upon his wife's "report card" then he will become defensive because he doesn't want to lose any ground regarding his self-worth. In this example, it doesn't mean Bob becomes a mute and never says anything. It means if he leans fully upon his Father and not upon his own understanding then genuine fruit of the Spirit will be produced. Bob may actually use his intellect, articulation skills and his knowledge of scripture but it will come through the timing, prompting and guidance of the Holy Spirit. If it comes through his direction then the timing will be off, he will be prompting out of fear and be guided by his human spirit. This stage of the recovery can often be the most difficult because we don't want to be dependent upon anyone and that includes God. This stage is difficult because it goes to the core and origin of our sinful nature. Adam and Eve wanted to be independent from God and direct their own lives. The truth of the matter is we make very poor gods. The recovering sex addict becomes aware of this nature through and how his nature was exacerbated in the thorn of his addiction. As the pain of his brokenness subsides, he forgets what this independence from God cost him and he returns to directing his own life through his strengths and abilities. I recently had a conversation with a recovering sex addict I had seen 5 years ago in an intensive workshop. He had remained sober and intimate with God and his wife for over 3 years before he relapsed into having affairs. In looking back, he was now aware his pride and self-confidence had gradually replaced his dependency upon God. God will allow hardships, difficulties, and persecutions into a recovering addict's life in order to keep him in the place of depending upon Him. Addict's who learn to embrace the second blessing of this thorn mature into tremendous testimonies of God's power.

A couple of years ago, a man who had been attending my group for over a year, died suddenly of a heart attack at an early age. His sexual sin had cost him his marriage and strained his relationships with his children and his extended family. His life was going through a period of hardships and difficulties that were a natural consequence of his sinful behavior. I had watched him embrace his thorn in the flesh and receive the washing of God's sufficient Grace. I watched him consistently hold his heavenly father's hand in his realization he was weak and could not lean upon his own understanding. The result of this process was a man who had a peace that surpassed his current situation. This peace affected those around him because it was a blessing from God and not self-manufactured. Because it was a supernatural peace, others were blessed and God received the glory. During his last group, he reviewed what God had done in his life during that year and his on-going love and concern for his wife and children. He closed our group with prayer. The last words I heard him say were spoken to his heavenly Father. His teenage son was with him when he died and reported he raised his hands over his head and then went to be with the Lord. I like to believe he was reaching up to hold his Daddy's hands which lead him into his eternal home.

The Israelites, once leaving Egypt, had to experience the hardships and difficulties of desert life before they were ready to receive the blessing of God to enter the promise land. They may have felt God had left them hanging. The Israelites had a slave mentality that created dependency upon the slave master. The master told them when to eat, sleep, work, worship and often when to die. They had given up hope of ever being free and surrendered their wills to the control of the slave master. God could have delivered them directly to the Promise Land but they needed to learn things one can only learn through taking a journey of hardships. The journey of the sex addict is very similar. He has a slave mentality which created a dependency upon his master of sexual addiction. This master took control of every aspect of his life. He gives up all hope he will ever be delivered and finally reaches a point of despair. When the Egyptians released the Israelites, the people were more than happy to follow Moses and did just what he said without complaining. Before long they are backed up against the sea with Pharaoh's chariots breathing down their necks. Exodus 14:12 the people said, *"Didn't we say to you in Egypt, leave us alone; let us serve the Egyptians? It would have been better for us to serve the Egyptians than to die in the desert!"* If you review God's interactions with the Pharaoh and the Egyptians, it was God who hardened their hearts. He did this so he would get the glory and so all the world would see how great God is. In their first difficulty, hardship, and persecution event, they wanted to return back to slavery because it was familiar and all they had known for 400 years. When we are frightened, we want to return to what is familiar and predictable because we find a strange security in that place even when it involves slavery. The Israelites had to learn to experience total dependency upon God for their every need. The recovering sex addict will need to experience the same type of journey in order to develop a full and complete reliance upon God. At the beginning of the addict's journey of recovery, he is willing to do whatever it takes to be healed because of the pain of his brokenness. The Pharaoh was an evil man that was partnered with the devil and in direct opposition of God. God, however, took what Satan intended for evil and used for his good and glory. The Israelites continued to experience more hardships and difficulties as they journeyed into the wilderness. They experienced the hardships of poor water, no water, limited food supply, boring food and relapse into idolatry. Sometimes these difficulties came as a means of discipline so they would correct their "flight path" of self-direction and renew their dependency upon him. After many years of wilderness life, they were allowed to cross over into the promise land. Some days the recovery process feels very boring and repetitive. The recovering addict may become tired of the daily provision of God's "manna" and longs for the excitement of his past sinful life. He will learn perseverance through these dry "desert days" of recovery. Eventually, the Israelites were allowed to cross the Jordan River and into the promise land. Once across, they stacked 12 stones that had been taken from the river's floor. These were meant to be stones of remembrance. Whenever someone would pass by these stones in the coming years, they would be reminded what God had done that day. The recovering sex addict, who is willing to walk out the hardships of recovery, can become stones of remembrance for future generations. His children and even great-grandchildren can look back at his life and say that "this was a Godly man who trusted and leaned upon the Lord." I often ask a recovering addict what he would give to know that his future generations will say this about him. The correct answer is "everything." The giving of that "everything" includes the surrendering of the addict's self-direction and fully submitting to the leading of the Spirit. The revival that begins with the addict's broken and contrite spirit and is renewed through God's Truth penetrating to his inner most part, will not only effect those close to him but also the generations to come. King David's greatest failure, his sexual sin with Bathsheba, produced his son Solomon and through that lineage came the Savior of the world. What if Nathan refused to obey God's prompting to confront his king because he was more afraid of David than God? What if David had stayed in the place of secrecy and he continued to experience his "bones wasting away" torment he described in Psalm 32? What if David didn't walk out the restoration process described in Psalm 51 because it became too difficult? The fact is Nathan was obedient to God, he did confront David about his sin, David did not stay in a place of torment and secrecy, and he chose to walk through the difficult path of restoration. This path David walked out began in a place where Satan intended evil and destruction for a "man after God's own heart" but ended in God receiving the glory. The end result became a "standing stone" monument to God's powerful Grace and Mercy. The same power that held back the Jordan River years ago is the same power which restored David and can restore the sexually addicted today. If this process had not occurred then there would not have been the "standing stone" of Psalm 51. There would not have been the wonderful writings of Solomon. How many people have been changed through the generations because of this process occurring, we will never know the answer on this side of eternity. If the recovering sex addict choices the path of restoration then I believe the same impact can occur in the generations to follow.

You may be the "Nathan" in the sex addict's life. Will you be willing to be used by God to be a man of Truth and Grace? Or will you fear the addict's response more than fearing and respecting God? Will you listen to the shame that says you are not worthy to be used by God to confront sin? Maybe you are the sexual addict. Do you believe God's Grace is sufficient to cover your sins or do you believe you have exceeded his mercy and grace? Are you still protecting your sin through rationalization because you still enjoy your sin and it hasn't cost you enough? You can choice today if your sexual sin has cost you enough. You can choice the same path David chose and embrace your thorn of sexual addiction. David was a man. He was not divine and he did not have supernatural powers which allowed him to see into the future. He was a man. Just like any other man. He had to choose. He chose the hard path of restoration. He could have chosen the easy path and followed his sinful nature. Praise God he did not. Whether you are asked to be a Nathan today or you are the sexual addict, you will have to choose each day which path you will take. I have always been a big fan of Joshua. I like his attitude. He had a righteous warrior's attitude. I believe this attitude was demonstrated in Joshua 24:15. Even at the end of his life that attitude came through when he challenged the people to "choose for themselves whom they would serve...but as for me and my household, we will serve the Lord." His attitude said "you need to fish or cut bait". Is today the day you make that chose to be a legacy for generations or will you return to your false gods of sexual idolatry? Ask God to give you this day the same attitude and empowerment that he gave Joshua so many years ago. Choose.

Chapter 8
The Pursuit of Purity and Holiness
Establishing Effective Accountability

The goal of this chapter is to provide steps for beginning and maintaining effective accountability. Some of the information will be a review of concepts we covered in previous chapters. Recovering from sexual addiction can be overwhelming especially in the beginning. Accountability is a key component of the maturation process of a Christian and essential to the addicts' healing and recovery journey. If accountability is viewed as overwhelming or ineffective then many recovering addicts will lose heart and cease using it. The primary objective of this chapter is to provide a user friendly and effective system for accountability. These techniques can be utilized in other areas of our lives where we might struggle with deeply rooted issues or strongholds. If you are setting up accountability systems within your church then these steps would be helpful in establishing structured accountability which promotes our dependency upon the Lord. If your men of grace are in place then have them read this chapter first as means of helping them understand this process. My hope is you will be able to utilize these biblically based techniques and practically apply them to your recovery process.

Visualize in the far distance a mountain whose peak reaches high into and beyond the canopy of the tallest clouds. The mountain is steep and appears treacherous should anyone attempt to scale its lofty heights. There are other points of interest in this mountain range which exist at lower altitudes than this snow covered peak. As you lower your focus away from the peak you notice the lower points seem to descend like a huge staircase. Eventually you gaze upon the base of the mountain where the terrain is flat, green and inviting in appearance with the leisure lifestyle it surely must provide. As you continue to adjust your focus, you notice the small dots on the mountain are actually people. The largest concentration of these dots, or people, appear along the base and they become more scattered and fewer in number as the mountain ascends into the clouds. You admire the brave sojourners who ventured away from the safety of the base camp and now slowly climb the dangerous trail to reach the pinnacle. You wonder what kind of courage it must take to make this climb and doubt you could ever begin the journey away from the safety and comfort of the flat lands.

The word picture I have just described is one which exemplifies the journey of the Christian within this fallen world. When you set out on a journey to a place you have never been then you might enter the address into your GPS before you leave. Without this address or destination point you might just wonder around aimlessly until you ran out of gas or your car died. The same is true when we become a Christian. We need a destination point which is a fixed position and not one that changes based upon our emotions, external pressures or cultural trends. There is a constant pressure within our world to comply, blend in and never ever make anyone else feel uncomfortable through our actions or words. This pressure will in turn promote the use of compromise regarding our principles and integrity. Let's return to our imagery of the mountain. The mountain peak represents our destination point for us as Christians. It is the address which is placed within our spirit upon the event of our salvation. This address or destination is called *Holiness* or *Purity*. Let me clarify something from the very beginning. I did not say perfection or perfectionism. I said holiness and purity. The pursuit of perfectionism most often leads to legalism, pride, self-glorification as well as shame, despair and hopelessness. When we become a Christian, we enter into the process known as sanctification. This is a process where we are being transformed and set aside for a holy purpose. This process will also promote us decreasing in self-reliance and increasing in God dependency. This process is lead and directed by the Holy Spirit and our responsibility is to submit and surrender our will to this transforming journey.

Destination: Purity and Holiness

Let us take a few moments to describe some the points of interest in our visualized mountain. The highest peak represents Holiness and Purity. This fixed point is what we set our spiritual GPS upon. It is what we regain our baring with when we venture off the path and loose our way. Have you ever made a wrong turn when traveling under the direction of your GPS? It will inform you it is "recalculating" and once it has done this it usually gives you instructions in how to make a "u" turn. The same is true with the conviction of the Holy Spirit. He always keeps His sight upon the destination of Holiness and warns us when we get off the path. Repentance occurs when we respond, follow His directions, make the "u" turn and get back on the right path. I have often turned off my GPS because I believed I knew a better way to go and its persistent demands for me to turn around frustrated me so I just turned it off. Many Christians will find the demands of pursuing purity to be too great and believe they know a better and easier way to get to the summit. I have done this many times in my own journey. I would come to certain scriptures or teachings I found distasteful or displeasing and would look for a way around them. This became apparent early in my journey when I was challenged by the scripture which required me to submit to my father's authority. I didn't have a problem submitting to anyone else in authority but I rebelled against my father. I justified me taking a different path than God required because I was a pretty good guy in all the other areas and I had judged my father as not being worthy of my submission. I turned off my Holy Spirit GPS conviction and continued on my own way. I eventually ran into a brick wall of brokenness and surrendered to God's recalculating and bringing me back to His Truth and the requirement to submit to my earthly father's authority. I'd like to say it was the only time I ever shut off the Holy Spirit GPS but we don't have enough time to cover all of them. The thing I learned with each repentance and turn around in my life was my enteral Father still loved me and knew what was best for me even when it meant a difficult path.

Let's return to our mountain scene. I mention the mountain range before us also has lowering points of interest which descend in a stair step fashion. These points represent a pattern of compromise.

Before we ever start the journey, we notice and have heard from others before us that the trip to the pinnacle of Holiness and Purity is difficult and dangerous. We notice the small dots of people in the higher elevations often slip, slide and sometimes fall. We place this in contrast with the large group of people at the bottom who appear to not have a care in the world and never seem to struggle with slip, slides or falls. Before we ever take out on the journey, we adjust our sights to one of the lower points of which we believe we can conquer without much threat of slip, sliding or falling. We compare our journey to those who live the life of worldliness at the base and those who have set their goal upon lower points than you. Through this comparison, we believe we are on the right path and carry some spiritual pride in the path we have chosen. As we start our journey we realize this path is difficult as well and contains slip, slides and falls. We notice the lower points and determined God has given us a new calling or direction. If we continue in this pattern we will find we have made ourselves at home at the base of the mountain. Your compromises beget more compromises. It does not promote integrity, principles or perseverance. When one generation takes its focus off of Holiness and pursues compromise then the next generation picks up right where the last one stopped. We live in a world where generational compromises have left the church living just above or right with the base camp of worldly living. In other words, we don't look any different than the rest of the world. Revival is a word the church has used for various purposes throughout the years. Some use it to announce a special meeting entitled Revival Meeting. This involves a special preacher, extra time and sometimes a unique place. Most churches have a scheduled revival meeting set in their yearly planning calendar months before the event occurs. There is nothing wrong with having these group events and many people have come to know the Lord in these services. I do believe; however, most revivals begin with an individual. It starts with one person being convicted to turn away from a life of compromise and set their sights upon purity and holiness. When one person, through the power of His Spirit, begins to move away from the group of compromisers then 2 things can occur. Some will follow and others will ridicule. There is an old song which contains the line "sit down, sit down, sit down cause you rocking the boat." As humans, we tend to seek comfort and avoid discomfort at most any cost. We are comfortable when sermons, songs and fellowship are light whimsical entertaining events that are kept within the walls of the church. We become uncomfortable when sermons, songs and fellowship convict and challenge us to grow and be a light unto the world 7 days a week. If God calls you to pursue Holiness, then some of the people who want you to stop "rocking the boat" of compromise, may live in the same house with you or sit on the same pew. Let me interject, pursuing Holiness is not preaching or evangelizing. Very few of us are called to this assignment but we are all called to Holiness. As God begins to work this revival within you and this becomes actions or Fruit of the Spirit, then the revival may spread to others who want to follow this same path. These people will become an important part of your journey as you will assist each other as you experience slip, slides and falls throughout your ascent to Holiness.

1 Peter 1:13-16 *[13] Therefore gird up the loins of your mind, be sober, and rest your hope fully upon the grace that is to be brought to you at the revelation of Jesus Christ; [14] as obedient children, not conforming yourselves to the former lusts, as in your ignorance; [15] but as He who called you is holy, you also be holy in all your conduct, [16] because it is written, "Be holy, for I am holy."* (NKJV)

Peter witnessed the ultimate example of holiness every day for 3 years. In spite of this intimate walk with Jesus, he continued to have slips, slides and falls back into his old behavior. In spite of these relapses, Jesus redeemed and restored him. It wasn't until Pentecost that Peter became enlightened by the power of the Holy Spirit. It was at this point he began his pursuit of Holiness. Peter was never perfect in his performance and had some slips and slides but regained his bearings and continued in his pursuit. Years passed and the Spirit moved him to pen the words recorded in 1 Peter 1:13-16. Peter lived in a time when the pursuit of Holiness could cost you your life. Tradition says Peter was crucified upside down because he believed he was unworthy to be crucified in the same manner as Christ. Few believers today will face death in their pursuit of Holiness but the call Peter gave us 2,000 years ago is still the same for us today no matter what the cost. Paul was quoting a verse from Leviticus that God spoke repeatedly to His first covenant chosen people. The people of the old testament only had frail examples of Holiness behavior, did not have his written word and were ministered to periodically through the use of His prophets. New testament followers have the example of Christ's life, His written word and the indwelling of His Spirit. With these things in place we should make no excuse in striving for Holiness.

So, why should we pursue Holiness and why is Peter quoting some accent verse from the book of law? First and most importantly, it is a command and not a suggestion. God's commands are always based upon His love for us and what is best for His children. As humans, we desire the easy path but God knows the best path for us and it can be difficult at times. For too long we have permitted generational compromises to occur. We have become the church of Laodicea. We look really good on the outside but we are lukewarm in our faith. We have created seeker friendly churches that care more about people's feelings than preaching the word of God. We have lowered the bar regarding sexual integrity, the sanctity of life and holiness of marriage. Revival will not begin in the lost until His children are awakened and revived. This revival begins with the one Christian saying "Father, let it begin with me." Will you be that person who accepts the challenge to pursue Holiness and Purity? If you are then, maybe, we can begin a new generational pattern where those to come will look back at the legacy of Holiness we set for them.

In the next few pages we will discuss the practical applications of pursuing Holiness and Purity, the role it plays in the recovery from sexual addiction and how to address the slip, slides and falls. This is not an easy journey and some will choose not to accept the challenges and difficulties of the pursuit. The information and challenges of this chapter are not intended to be a litmus test regarding your salvation. This information is intended to challenge those who are convicted to pick up their cross, follow the example of Christ's walk, and set your eyes upon the goal of Holiness.

You may have noticed that I have capitalized Holiness and Purity. The reason is these are the proper noun titles for the destination each of our Holy Spirit GPS's should be set upon. So, if you are ready. Let's begin the journey to Holiness and Purity.

Preparing for the journey

As with any journey there are certain steps of preparation which need to be in place prior to making the first step. Without these things in place you will become discouraged, weary, and eventually give up. You may add to this list elements you deem helpful for your particular journey but these are some things I have witnessed as essential keys for long term success. These steps are not in any particular order of importance.

Support and accountability

The followers of Christ in the first century church did not pursue Holiness alone. They had brothers and sisters of faith to encourage, pray for, guide and challenge them. In most branches of the military they have groups of specially trained men and women who are often referred to as special forces. You will need to find and train these special group of men and woman for your support army and for the battles you will experience alone the journey. I refer to these people as men/women of grace. It is best these special people be of your same sex. The men/women of grace should have these minimal qualities: Christian, safe, truthful, available, point you toward God reliance and never self-reliance, and demonstrate a working understanding of grace, mercy and forgiveness. If you do not have these people in your life right now, then start today searching for them. I cannot stress this enough, you will not be able to do this journey alone. It is ok to ask for help in this search. Go where they might congregate such small groups, classes or support groups. Ask your pastor to direct you toward someone who meets these criteria. These men/women of grace will perform 2 functions. They will provide accountability and they will meet needs. Let me give you a working definition for accountability. Accountability is the process of establishing external discipline in areas of your life where you lack internal discipline. Let me give you an example. If you lack internal discipline regarding the use of your eyes and lusting after women then you need external discipline through accountability. This support team also meets needs. You will need encouragement, validation and affirmation throughout your journey. You will need someone to come along side you when you fall to promote the healing atonement of God's mercy and grace. You will need to be challenged and "sharpened" to get up and continue when you have slide. Without Barnabas's encouragement then Saul may have never grown into Paul. Timothy needed Paul's fathering love and direction to address his spirit of fear and step into his calling.

Develop an understanding of holiness and purity

It may sound odd or simplistic but many Christians do not have an understanding of what holiness and purity are. The perfect example of this would obviously be through studying the walk and teachings of Christ. There are also numerous examples in scripture of men and women who pursued Holiness and also fell. David is a great example of a man after God's own heart but fell horribly into sexual sin and murder. We also see God's provision of restoration and healing for David in Psalm 51. Ask your pastor for references on studies or teachings about holiness and purity. If you are going to set your GPS upon a destination, then it helps to know what it looks like.

Identify the obstacles which will cause slips, slides and falls during your journey

Throughout your life, you may have experienced repeated sinful patterns. Sometimes they reoccur with regular frequency while others are sporadic in occurrence. You might even say "I can't remember when I didn't struggle with this." In most cases these struggles are things that are deeply rooted within our soul and sinful nature. These struggles have created slips, slides and falls in your past attempts at pursuing Holiness. These struggles will and do not disqualify you from the pursuit of Holiness. On the contrary, these struggles can actually strengthen your walk by promoting a God reliance and not a self-reliance. They do, however, need to be identified. Because of the focus this book, the example we will use for the struggle will be the affliction of sexual temptation. This process can also be used in dealing with any reoccurring struggle. Here are some examples of other struggles: pride, self-reliance, anger, lying, gossiping, approval addiction, legalism, and passive-aggressive behavior. Wouldn't it be great if our children had the tools to deal with slip, slides and falls before they occurred? My hope is parents will utilize these teachings in raising their children and equipping them with Godly tools in their life coping tool box. Think how much different your life would have been if someone had taught you how to deal with your many failures of adolescence.

Understand who you are:

Most Christians today do not know who they truly are. As mentioned in previous chapters, we live in a world that defines us by our performance. As Christians, we are defined by Christ's performance and redemptive works. If who we are is based upon our performance, then we are in trouble. Our identity will be tentative at best. It will lack security because it will be controlled by the vacillations of our successes and failures. When we walk in agreement with who we are in Christ then we carry the security of knowing nothing can separate us from His love. That includes our own failures. If you are willing to take on the pursuit of Holiness, then you need to know you will sometimes fall and fail in your performance. Jesus has already fully paid for those failures upon the cross. He has also given us a system by which we can be redeemed and healed when those falls occur. This system of honesty, grace, mercy and forgiveness separates our failed performance from who we really are. If you attempt this journey basing your identity upon your performance, then all you are doing is picking up more shame and guilt. With these additional burdens, you will eventually quit.

Releasing burdens

When we go on a difficult journey we need to first cast off the things which will burden, impede and halt our progress. Most of us carry the shame and guilt of past falls and failures. Most of us carry lies that are wrapped around the spirit of fear. You cannot set your eyes upon the goal ahead of you when you are always looking back. When we carry these burdens of guilt, shame, fear and lies, Satan uses them to tell us we are unworthy and unable to make this climb. It does not mean you must be free from all the burdens of this world before you begin. That would be the pursuit of perfection. It means we need to be in the process of addressing these burdens.

Spiritual warfare

2 Corinthians 10:4-5 have been a reoccurring theme throughout this book. This is a battle. Not a battle against other people but against principalities and ultimately against the author of lies, Satan himself. We need to know the enemy and his tactics in order to defeat him. This journey will be one which strengthens and conditions us to defeat the enemy through the might of God. Part of doing battle is knowing where the battle line exists. If your enemy controls the battle line then you will always be in a defensive stance and at a disadvantage. As mighty warriors for the Lord, we will determine where the battle line will be because where ever you draw the line is where the battle will be. One of the most familiar Christian battle cry hymns is *Onward Christian Soldiers*. We will take the battle to the

enemy and we will decide where the battle line will be. Some of us have lost ground to the enemy during previous conflicts. You may have lost your integrity due to persistent falls into pornography. You will be practicing effective spiritual warfare throughout this journey of recovery. Within that process God will restore, redeem and reclaim territory that the enemy has taken. Your integrity can and will be reclaimed because our God is just that mighty.

Develop a warrior's attitude

Part of being an effective warrior means developing a warrior's attitude. Many of us have spent years beating ourselves up through regret of past sins and failures. In some cases, this leads us in attempting to replace Jesus on the cross as we bludgeon our souls with self-hatred. In other situations, we blame others as the root for all our despair. Neither one of these approaches glorifies God. Satan is the author of lies and the promoter of our despair. When we begin to realize the true enemy then we can develop a warrior's attitude that says "no more." No more will Satan assault me with the lies of fear and shame. No more will he molest my soul with the delusional fantasy world of sexual sin. This attitude draws a line in the sand and says "No more and my Father is bigger and more powerful than your lies, obstacles and temptations." This climb and pursuit is not for quitters, losers or lukewarm believers. Satan manipulates us into quitting, believing we are losers and settling into staying put. We are overcomers and children of the King of all kings. Now let's strap on a Godly warrior's attitude and kick Satan's butt.

Setting up accountability and dealing with slip, slides and falls

In the battle with sexual addiction, finding and establishing effective accountability is paramount. Many recovering addicts will lose heart and become discouraged because they do not know what to look and ask for from their men of grace. It is beneficial to have questions these men will ask you periodically throughout each week. Let us begin with one simple but effective question, "Did you have any slip, slides or falls this week?" Before these questions can be utilized we first need to define their meaning.

What are slips?

Very simply put, slips occur in our head. Slips occur when either new input is taken in or old input is recalled. New input comes into our thoughts through our input centers, better known as our eyes and ears. In other words, a slip occurs when you either see or hear a sexually charged stimuli. This stimulus is one that has the potential to trigger your particular relationship with sexual sin. In other words, what is a trigger for you may not be one for someone else and vice versa. Part of your recovery plan will be identifying your particular triggers. Once this new input comes into your brain, you have a multitude of options regarding the next step. You can try to ignore it. You can minimize it by saying it is not a big deal. You can maximize it by proclaiming it to be the biggest sin ever committed. You can store it away in the recesses of your mind to be utilized later with fantasy and acting out. Here is the option I recommend. This new input or "slip" is actually an opportunity to practice spiritual warfare.

This is where you get to practice 2 Corinthians 10:5 by taking this thought captive and bringing it into obedience. This will take practice and more practice. You may have spent your whole life practicing the afore mentioned options, so be patient will yourself.

A similar process may occur when old images or thoughts are recalled. Because sexual images and experiences are so powerful, they are often "burned" into our brains. These images and experiences are tucked away in the recesses of our brain like a forgotten file in your computer. These "files" can pop open at any time during the recovery and healing process. They can even occur in your dreams. We will utilize the same process to deal with old images and memories as with the new input.

Let me state something extremely important here. These mental slips are not sins. I will say it again. Slips are not sinning. It is what we do with these slips that determine if it becomes a slide and a fall into sinful behavior. Let me prove my point. When Jesus was tempted by Satan, he heard, saw and most likely could smell everything presented to him but yet he did not sin. We live in a sexually fallen world and we will see and hear things we do not seek out. You see, we are moving the battle line away from the "I'm about to sin" boundary. Where ever you draw the line is where the battle will be. If we move the line away from the threat and pressure of "I'm about to sin" then we become more empowered to kick Satan's butt. Many men in recovery view slips as sinful and therefore they become "opportunities" to shame themselves with the messages of failure. Let me repeat this one more time. Slips are opportunities to practice spiritual warfare and not to shame yourself.

Let me give you a practical example of how this would work with a man of grace. The man of grace asks "Did you have any slip, slides or falls this week?" The recovering addict replies "I had several slips this week, some were more difficult than others but I was able to take them captive and none of them became slides or falls." The man of grace "Good job, I'm proud of the victories you had this week." Remember these men do 2 things, they provide external discipline, encouragement and also meet needs. Along with accountability he also had his needs of affirmation, validation and encouragement in being a godly man and warrior.

What are slides?

When slips are left unattended then they have the ability to slide into our hearts unabated. Remember when we discussed the issue of the addiction being addressed as a thorn in our spiritual flesh? How we take part of this spiritual flesh and we compartmentalize and protect it from the process of sanctification? When we have said "yes" to our flesh repeatedly then there is no "muscle strength" or resistance built up against these slides. When the "slip" image or input is left un-assaulted then it will slide into my heart where we will consume it with lust and covetousness. Lust is about using something or somebody and coveting is taking something which is not mine to use in the first place. At this point, there has been no acting out behavior but now we have sinned against God.

Matthew 5:28 **But I say to you that whoever looks at a woman to lust for her has already committed adultery with her in his heart.**

Jesus could not have made it anymore clearer when he spoke this truth. At a minimum, the slide has violated 2 of the 10 Commandments. So, how do we deal with a slide? We address it with truth and grace. We acknowledge the truth we have sinned against God and seek His mercy which is offered through the gracious works of His Son. Once we have asked for his forgiveness then we need to return to dealing with our thoughts and practice spiritual warfare. The image or thought which slid into the heart will need to be taken captive as well as the possibility of the issue of shame and guilt. Whether it be a slip, slide or fall it is never an opportunity to shame ourselves. Shame does not produce change.

Let's once again look at how this would work with a man of grace. "Did you have any slip, slides or falls this week?" "I had several slips I was able to battle through. There was, however, the one situation at work that became a slide, where I lingered too long and had lustful thoughts about a co-worker." The man of grace responses with "Have you ask God to forgive you for the lusting? If not let's do it right now. Have you brought those thoughts into obedience? Now, what did you learn from this and what can you put in place so it does not repeat itself?" The pattern the man of grace is following now is this: *Truth-Grace-Challenge*. The *truth* is his partner sinned against God. He didn't make a mistake. He sinned. Secondly, he pointed him toward *forgiveness and grace*. The sin must first be separated from the sinner before he can be *challenged* to assess his behavior and what he learned. If the grace and forgiveness is not applied then the process is shaming because he is still carrying the burden of his sin. The man of grace will be there next week to see if he follows through with his plan. He could validate and encourage him to keep up the good fight. Once again, slides are opportunities to grow in our understanding of His sufficient grace and practice spiritual warfare.

What are falls?

Let me take you back to the illustration of climbing the mountain and setting our spiritual GPS upon the peak or goal of holiness and purity. Along this climb you will have slips. When slips occur, you will need to stop, practice spiritual warfare, catch your barring, learn from what caused the slip and reset your GPS to continue in the journey. You don't lose any ground or fall backwards. Sometimes in the journey you slide. In addressing this slide, you need to attend to the afore mentioned steps plus you slide backwards and need to regain the ground through seeking first God's grace, mercy and forgiveness. Other times in our pursuit of the peak of purity, we will fall. In addressing falls, we need to address and apply the steps mentioned in dealing with slips and slides plus now we are injured and we have injured those close to us. There needs to be healing.

Slips and slides left unattended will eventually lead to falls. Sometimes these falls occur because we store up the pleasurable new sexually charged input or continue to reminisce about the sex events of the past. Other times, falls occur because the recovering person continues to shame themselves and falls into old sexual acting out as a way to escape or medicate this pain. Finally, falls occur because we have spent years creating "ruts" or cycles in our brains that promote persistent acting out behavior. Early in recovery, the addict has not had time for his heart and brain to heal. His brain believes sexual activity is a "number one food group." In other words, he believes he must have sex or he will not survive. I am not giving permission for addicts to have falls. Our goal is to move the battle line away from this area and into spiritual warfare or dealing with slips. This, however, takes time.

I will always lean in the direction of being honest. I also realize being honest sometimes carries very real life consequences. I bring this topic up now because when an addict falls or relapses into sinful sexual behavior, I will encourage them to be honest with the people they have hurt in doing so. This choice is always the recovering addicts to make. This is never more evident when it comes to the effect a relapse has upon a marriage. The spouse may have already informed her husband she will never tolerate him returning to his acting out behavior. She has informed him the consequence will be a divorce. Other consequences can result in loss of employment, separation from children and in some cases jail time. As I have already mentioned, I would never advocate dishonesty but it is only fair the recovering addict understands the possible consequences. In many cases, his desire to be obedient to the Lord and his pursuit of purity is more important than returning to a life of lies. A man of grace accountability partner may also establish in the beginning he will not accept dishonesty when it comes to sexual falls. He is not pressuring or threatening the recovering addict but maintaining his own integrity and principles. Others may choose to stay involved no matter what.

Most addicts have had repeated falls until they hit brokenness. At start of recovery they will need a time of healing. This healing time means spending the primary focus upon being soaked in God's word, connecting with men of grace and taking a sexual fast. If they are married, then the same is true for the spouse. She will need time to grieve, forgive, soak in God's word, connect with women of grace and take a sexual fast. This healing will begin with them individually and then over time move into marriage counseling. If the recovering addict has a sexual fall or relapse and chooses to be honest with his spouse then the same steps should be applied.

The man of grace's response to confessed sexual fall should be everything covered under slips and slides plus the challenge to be honest. Remember the order is: Truth-Grace-Challenge. His challenge may sound something like this "Ok, you can rest in that God has forgiven you. Now, what does God require of you regarding your wife?" This may sound harsh or pressuring but the bottom line is "It does not matter what we think." God is the author of truth and not us. It has been my observation, men who choose not to be honest with their wife regarding falls, at best, have a marriage which survives but does not thrive. Most men who choose this path are eventually found out and their marriage doesn't survive the dishonesty. It other words, it wasn't the fall that killed the marriage, it was the dishonesty. As I have said more than once, I encourage and promote honesty.

This has been a fairly lengthy discussion regarding slide, slides and falls but the set up should be fairly simple. If you are the recovering addict and you have found some men of grace then have them read this chapter so they can understand their role. My hope is this will become a process men engage with their son's during their practice time for manhood which is often referred to as adolescence. My hope also is this could become a process by which we deal with any repeated sin. Practicing these techniques helps us to get tools in our life skills tool box. They are intended to point us toward Christ, become more dependent upon Him and learn how a Godly man/woman deals with the slip, slides and falls in the pursuit of holiness and purity.

Chapter 9

Final Thoughts

Steps taken by one man to break the cycle of sexual sin:

"Everyone's battle with sexual sin is different, but if you are struggling with this specific sin, I hope that my story will encourage you and give you HOPE that change is possible. Here are the steps as they happened to me:

Step #1 - I began to pray "God, I am so sick of having this sin in my life and I am asking that You do WHATEVER it takes to rip it from me". If you are NOT willing to pray this same prayer, please don't waste your time reading the rest of this testimony because you are not ready. I had to face the harsh reality that even though I always felt bad about my sin, I still enjoyed it and I "protected" my sin. The fact is, I was unable to stop my sex sin cycle and I was unable to change. Only GOD was able to change me. But in order for that to happen, I had to get out of His way. So, if you can't say "God, please do WHATEVER it takes", then you are still in the phase of denial or unwilling to give up the sin.

Step # 2 - I confessed ALL my sexual sins to a couple of trustworthy friends AND my wife (I probably would recommend that you do step #3 before step #2. This is the order in which it happened for me so that is why I'm putting this as step #2, but depending on your situation, step #3 should be next). This step of confession is absolutely required and is the crucial step that I had always skipped in the past. My cycle would be as follows: sexual sin, guilt, pray for forgiveness, promise to God and myself that it will never happen again, passage of various lengths of time (sometimes a few months and sometimes only a few hours), and then I would give in to my sexual sin again and start the cycle all over. Over the years, the "cycle" became more predictable with triggers such as stress or boredom and for me, my sexual sins became more severe. Breaking the sexual sin cycle is often very different than other sins or addictions due to the deeply hidden nature of sexual sin, shame associated with the behavior, and fear of losing reputation or relationships. I completely understand the thoughts of "If anyone finds out, I will be hated", "My wife will never forgive me", or "I will lose everything I love including my wife and kids". Here is another harsh reality I had to realize: __MY RELATIONSHIP WITH GOD IS MORE IMPORTANT THAN ANYTHING ELSE ON EARTH INCLUDING MY WIFE AND KIDS.__ *I know that is a difficult statement to handle but it is the truth and it was time for me to grow up and obey God even if I had to go thru some hard times in other relationships. If you are willing to trust God to take over and do whatever is necessary (see step # 1), then you also have to be willing to trust HIM to handle and restore your other relationships as well (and possibly make those relationships better than ever before).*

Step # 3 - Get professional help. If your car breaks down and you are not a mechanic, you go see an expert. If your heat doesn't work at your house, you call an expert. Experts have experience for diagnosing the problem and specialized tools to properly repair what is broken. Someone that continues to tries to repair their car or heater on their own and the problem keeps recurring but yet refuses to get professional help is not very smart and for a very long time, I was an idiot. I kept thinking "I can fix it", "I can quit", "I got this". Thankfully, I finally call Jonathan Jones with Perfect Hope and he is definitely an expert. Jonathan knew exactly how to diagnose my specific cycle and pinpoint the triggers and most importantly helped me to implement a plan of attack. He did not allow me to make excuses or put a Band-Aid on my sin but yet, with love, Jonathan spoke God's truth and reminded me that God is calling me to be something different. He firmly helped me see clearly that "I ain't got this" and that Satan will continue to win the battle unless I humble myself and allow Almighty God to take over. Alone, I know that I would not have been able to change and none of the changes that have happened are my doing; however, God IS able and He DID change me and is continuing to change me daily into the man He designed me to be. Jonathan Jones is a powerful tool being used by God to rebuild many men that Satan has managed to break. If you are sick of your sexual sin, I beg you to call him. I promise if you will follow his expert advice, God will change you as well.

My battle for purity continues each day, but I promise you, there is hope. If you too are caught in sexual sin, DO NOT WAIT ANOTHER DAY. I beg you to take action TODAY.

Humbly and Sincerely.

Anonymous

Satan has used sexual temptation since the beginning of time to bring down Godly men, their families and whole nations.

Satan knows if the leaders of Christian homes fall then the home will fall. If the Christian homes fall then the communities fall. If the communities fall then eventually the nation will fall. I heard once we have become a nation which has forgotten how to blush. We no longer are grieved or shocked by the content of TV shows that minimize the effects of sexual sin. We have forgotten repentance means we turn away from sinful behavior. We have value the opinions of talk show hosts more than the word of God. We fear the disapproval of man and the labels of being called "intolerant and narrow minded" rather than speaking the truth. I spoke with a former pastor several years ago who had been the only conservative voice in a denomination which had embraced an extreme liberal view. He was a former pastor because Satan had used sexual temptation to destroy his lone voice of reason. Recently, in my state, a public official was forced to resign from his office because of an affair with a younger woman. He had clearly identified himself as a Christian, pro-life, family values politician who had taken many stances against liberal agendas. Satan used his oldest trick to take away his voice. The following day all the local "shock jock" disc-jockeys had made him the brunt of their jokes. We all know stories of this nature and experience a range of emotions when we hear these stories. We may feel angry and betrayed by these people and believe they got what they deserved. We may feel sadness and compassion for their families. The stories of the sexually fallen may be closer to home for some of you. It maybe you or a close loved one who has fallen into the snare of sexual sin. We all have a choice in how we respond to the

Christian man who falls into sexual sin. We can choose to "shoot our wounded" and feel justified in this action because they "reaped what they sowed." We can fix our stance in religious piety and cast the sinner from our midst. We can also minimize their sin and justify it by saying "boys will be boys". We can provide a quick fix formula prayer that puts their sin under the blood and never brought up again. In other words, we should never sever truth from grace. Truth without grace is a license to shoot the wounded. Grace without truth is a license to sin repeatedly. Both of these choices are the easy, quick and neat ways to deal with sexual sin. I heard a pastor of an inner-city church say "people business is messy and if you don't want to get messy stay away from people." Dealing with the sexual sin of fellow believers can and will get messy. There is no easy, quick and neat way to deal with it. I don't like people who are fear mongers. I don't want to use fear to try to manipulate or control anyone. The facts, however, are very clear and sometimes freighting. If we are not prepared to deal with the sexual sin of believers, then the church will fall. Through the years, I have witnessed God select specific churches to make them places of safety and revival for the sexual sinners. The healed sexual addict can be used by God to transform a church into a "real" church where the people can be open and transparent. This "real" church can show the world Christ came to deal with the messy stuff. These churches were willing to be used by God to do the "messy work" that comes with the recovery and healing process. Will your church or you as an individual be willing to be used by God for this purpose? My prayer is you will.

Maybe you are the one struggling with sexual addiction. You desire relief from the bondage of your sin but the shame tells you have sinned too greatly and are unworthy of God's mercy. You anguish for change but your fear drives you from your Master's place of peace and reassurance. Maybe you have tried to be honest with someone in the past and your honesty was met with rejection and condemnation. Maybe you have had hit bottom several times with repeated relapses and fear God has "turned you over" to your sinful desires. Maybe you still are enjoying your sexual sin and the only reason you read this book is to get someone off your back. You could have witnessed first-hand the "shooting" of the sexually wounded in your church or family. Your arrogance may still be telling you that you can still handle your relationship with your sexual sin. You may have even come up with a brand-new theology that promotes truth without grace or vice versa. Wherever you are God will meet you there. Sometimes you have to pray for God to give you the desire to have the desire to have the willingness for his change to occur. In other words, God will meet you where you are even if you haven't begun the healing process and have not hit bottom. You don't have to lose everything or anything else. You can choose today to seek the help you need.

Several years ago, I was given a book that was authored by a well know pastor who had written several books in the past. In the introduction part of this book he indicated this had been the most difficult book he had ever written. He believed every time he set down to write, he and his family came under spiritual attack. Over 10 years ago, God put upon my heart to write this book. I had already experienced a new appreciation for spiritual warfare when I begin dealing with sexual addiction. This attack intensified when this writing process began. I do not know what the result will be in putting these observations to paper but all I know is I had to be obedient to God. I do not say this as means of bragging or pointing to the amount of warfare which continues to this day. I bring this to the surface as a closing thought. Satan does not want to have this addiction exposed. He will attack you at every front to keep you and your family in bondage and shame. Do not attempt to fight this alone. Find a fellow believer who is safe and talk about your pain. The secrecy of this sin will keep you in bondage and shame. Ask God to show you today someone to talk with and take the risk to share your story. You will find you are not alone and God still loves you and can restore you.

About the author:

Jonathan D. Jones is the Founder and President of Perfect Hope. Perfect Hope is founded upon his teachings and through his over 40 years of counseling, mental health and ministry experience, Jonathan has developed unique techniques which address the heart of sexual sin. In 1999, he was called to address the issue of sexual sin within the church on a full-time basis. Since that time, he has developed intensive workshops, numerous workbooks, books, conferences and training institutes. He has witnessed hundreds of men walk in extended freedom from sexual sin with an improved intimacy with God and others. He has been married to his wife Jennifer for 35 years and they have 2 adult children. Jonathan has a Master's Degree in Counseling from Memphis State University. He is an ordained elder and long time Sunday school teacher. Jonathan's goal is to provide churches with biblically based tools to not only address the issue of sexual sin but to also improve Christians' intimacy with God.

About Perfect Hope:

Statement of faith

Perfect Hope is a Christian teaching and discipleship ministry created to empower, equip and support churches, families and individuals with biblically based tools in addressing the issue of sexual and relational sin.

Purpose Statement

To provide biblically based training, instruction and resources for the Christian community in addressing the plight of sexual and relational sin within the church. To address the barriers to intimacy with God through effective spiritual warfare and to promote the pursuit of holiness and purity.

Why the name Perfect Hope? Romans 5:5 tells of a hope that does not disappoint. When we place our hope in others, self or worldly pleasures then this hope will always disappoint. Jesus has and will always be the Perfect Hope which never disappoints.

Contact information:

You can find out more about Perfect Hope and its services at www.perfecthope.org or by calling 901-430-3412. You can also follow us on Facebook. You can email Jonathan at perfecthope.org@gmail.com